# The Urban
# Catholic University

# The Urban
# Catholic University

## by PAUL C. REINERT, S.J.

**Sheed and Ward    New York**

Standard Book Number: 8362–1379–3
Library of Congress Catalog Card Number: 73–113922

*Manufactured in the United States of America*

# Foreword

The title of this book is almost redundant, for most Catholic universities in the United States were founded in the cities and have distinct urban characteristics. Georgetown was first, founded in Washington in 1789, and was followed by St. Louis University (1818), and, eventually, by a Catholic university in virtually every city.

Only in recent years, however, has the Catholic university become truly urban-oriented, committed to the confrontation and solution of the problems of urban society. Without losing their distinctiveness as Catholic institutions, they have also become complete universities, embracing all disciplines and attracting an ever-increasing number of students and faculty of other religious faiths.

As president of one of these universities for the past twenty years, I have seen these trends develop, and naturally, have done considerable introspection and prediction. I have also, on occasion, expressed my thoughts before various audiences.

The speeches in this book have been delivered before edu-

*v*

cational conferences and university audiences. They reflect my conclusions on several key questions about the Catholic urban university:

—How does a college or university fulfill the double responsibility of offering a *bona fide*, quality higher educational program and at the same time provide the unique opportunities for total personal development which is the declared role of a Church-related institution?

—How does a college or university, situated in the heart of a large metropolitan area, grow and progress with its surrounding community, share its resources with its neighbors, and help the inner-city solve its cancerous problems of inequity, poverty, injustice and ignorance?

—How does a private, urban college or university attract substantial financial support from the wide variety of sources necessary to achieve its unique objectives?

All of these questions are intertwined, but they are dealt with in the three sections into which the speeches have been grouped.

I do not mean to suggest that these speeches provide unique or all-purpose answers, but they do, I believe, indicate the direction the Catholic urban university must take in realizing its purposes, old and new.

Inasmuch as these speeches were given over a long period of time, they may also have value in showing the evolution of trends, problems, and, hopefully, solutions.

PAUL C. REINERT, S.J.
*President*
*Saint Louis University*

# Contents

*The Urban*
*Catholic University*

# 1

# We Hold These Truths...?

"We hold these truths to be self-evident, that all men are created equal, that they are endowed by their Creator with certain unalienable rights . . ."

These important words of our American Declaration of Independence and also certain portions of our Constitution lay out the basic truths upon which we have erected our American way of life. From these documents immediately flow clear and definite obligations for those agencies in our society to whom we have committed the preservation and development of the life of free men. High in importance among these agencies we must place the school. And certainly American institutions of higher education have a most serious responsibility to use every means at their command to further specify and develop and transmit to new generations those basic truths which are the very foundation stones of our American democracy.

Every new American—and there were 11,734 new Americans born yesterday—comes into the world with certain birthrights that are part of his heritage as an American. I like to think that each American has certain birthrights as a person, as a member of the human race, and as a responsible agent. In each of these areas, American society has entrusted to education much of the duty of seeing that each individual receives his birthright whole and entire.

I am both heartened and disheartened by recent developments in higher education. Some of these developments threaten the transmission to the coming generation of their full American heritage. And the reason for this threat is the fact that American higher education is in danger of becoming depersonalized, decentralized, and devalued.

The explosive growth of American colleges and universities and the astounding rate of expansion anticipated in the coming decade pose special problems which threaten our traditional American concern for the dignity of the individual person. In the interest of coping with the onslaught, we have resorted to large classes. Closed-circuit television is beginning to reduce or eliminate the opportunity for self-expression and the cross-fertilization of class discussion. To satisfy our computers, we have reduced courses to a number and students to a hole in an IBM card. Some faculty actually complain about the presence of students in an institution that has as one of its principal purposes the transmission to the coming generation of the wisdom of the ages. Nor is this loss of concern for the person confined to big institutions. I have visited relatively small colleges where students complain of being treated as a number instead of as a person. They are stung by the impersonality of a fixed gaze from the professor whose lecture they have just heard. They wonder about the wisdom of status-seeking college presidents who authorize thousands for monumental structures and only hundreds for library books;

thousands for facilities for a few athletes, and little or nothing for the faceless thousands of students who are the fans in the stands; millions for bricks and mortar, but relatively little for warm-hearted men and women who will listen and understand. They look askance at faculty and administrative officers so completely preoccupied with securing the monetary rewards of their discipline and their profession that they have forgotten that it was the opportunity to inspire the youth of America that led them into educational work in the first place.

I have only sketched the problem, and probably over-generalized in doing so, but the danger is real. Respect for the individual person is clearly threatened. To offset this, we have tried to improve counseling—vocational, academic, and personal. We have elaborated our student personnel activities. We have used a hundred other means in an effort to reach the individual person and secure his fullest personal development in a well-balanced fashion. But we must redouble our efforts in the next ten years. For when all is said and done, these means are insufficient unless they are solidly founded in a basic attitude of respect and concern for the dignity of the student as a person, and a firm determination that he shall not be submerged in the mass, but treated as a fellow human being.

There is no incompatibility between a genuine and un-compromising dedication to scholarship, for students as well as faculty, and a simultaneous conviction that an education which we expect to be humanizing and liberalizing in its effects should also be human and liberal in its process. I think it is a major duty of all leaders in education to create among administrative officers, faculty, and staff not a sentimental attitude toward students, but a recognition of their dignity and importance to the purposes and destiny of the institution. It is the academic excellence, not of robots or of faceless members of a mass, but of human beings, of persons, that the college or university and its faculty exist to foster.[1]

Transmission of this birthright of our students to personal

treatment can never be accomplished by the isolated effort
of one person or even a few. It can be accomplished only by
a right attitude of mind and an elaborate concatenation of
practices which we have come to call "institutional press" or
"institutional thrust." Only the united conscious efforts of
administrative officers, faculty, and staff will guarantee that
each member of the coming generation will know by his own
experience the meaning of his God-given dignity as a person.

The second important threat confronting the birthrights of
our students is the danger that they will not receive their
full heritage as members of the human race, their full intellectual heritage from Western culture. We have created a
form of institutional organization and established norms in
its operation that, despite tremendous accomplishments,
threaten the transmission of our American heritage. I refer
to the ever-growing pressures resulting in segmentation and
isolation of the various disciplines, fragmentation of courses,
greater departmental autonomy. I refer to the widening gap
between scientists who speak in polysyllables and humanists
who speak in different polysyllables. I refer to the pressures
we have created for productive research to the detriment of
quality teaching. Plato said long, long ago: "What is honored
in a country is practiced there." Have the leaders of American
education honored some things too much? And others not
enough?

Do our students have the opportunity to see truth in all its
myriad manifestations—not just the truth that can be learned
through the electron microscope or the computer, but also
the truth which can never be learned in the laboratory, the
truth of man as he has lived in history, the truth of man's
nature as reflected in the great literatures of the world, the
truth of man's economic and social environment as the social
sciences have described him, the truth of man's relation to
everything in the universe as the world's great philosophers
have viewed it, the truth of man's relation to his Creator by
whom he has been endowed with "certain unalienable rights,"

among which are the right to "life, liberty, and the pursuit of happiness"?[2]

Have we, as responsible leaders of American education, seen to it that the youth of America receive their full birthright as human beings, as heirs of Western culture, as recipients of the American heritage? Or have we permitted our faculties to erect walls of separation even within the ivory tower? Have we, as responsible leaders of education, permitted the wholeness of truth to become so fragmented in the curriculum that it would take the wisdom of a Solomon even to see the connections, much less to integrate its parts?

Alfred North Whitehead once said, "The task of a University is the creation of the future." What kind of a future are we creating?

Is it by accident that recent attacks on American business education have fairly shouted for a solid core of liberal education? Is it without reason that all forms of professional education, including engineering and nursing, have sought more liberal development of their students?

Operating in an educational structure that certainly discourages, if it does not prevent, communication, we must take extraordinary means to create a climate of scholarly interchange. As educators, we have a clear obligation to find ways which will either modify the structure or overcome its bad effects. I refer to such administrative efforts as the Council of One Hundred at the University of Illinois, the encouragement of interdisciplinary approaches to learning, the development in the faculty of concern for total institutional impact on the student in addition to concern for his special discipline. Only by exercising active leadership in these areas can we be sure that young Americans will receive their full birthright to the education of free men.

An eminent philosopher and historian of philosophy, in a most perceptive analysis, has told us that today we are faced with a problem unique in the entire history of the human race: in the practicalities of life we have done away with God and in doing so have done away with all sound foundation for morality. It is not unique in human history that individuals and peoples and nations have violated the moral code. But it is unique that some nations have now formally declared with Nietzsche that "God is dead." The foundation for the moral code does not exist.[3] The completely logical conclusion of this is communism, where, since God no longer exists, the state is supreme and the individual derives his aims and purposes and whatever rights he has from the state.

But let us not point the finger of accusation at the Soviet Union until we have paused to examine our own consciences. The serious decline of morality in American life is everywhere evident. One need only mention catch phrases to conjure up the image: influence peddling, collusive bidding, payola, athletic scandals, juvenile delinquency, abortion mills. The pattern is not a pleasant one.

It is easy for us as educators to blame the home. It is easy for us to blame the churches. Yet I seriously question whether an educational system that professes to stand for all that America stands for can ignore foundations of morality, or can afford to forget the fact that our American Declaration of Independence forthrightly declares: "We hold these truths to be self-evident . . . that all men are endowed by their Creator with certain unalienable rights. . . ."

For in that statement we have the key difference between democracy, in which the state serves the individual and man derives his rights and duties from his Creator, and totalitarianism, in which the individual is the pawn of the state. We ignore at our peril the birthright of our students, as responsible decision makers, to learn the spiritual foundations of the American way of life.

Let us not naively assume that we are fooling the students in this matter. I recently had occasion to read a statement on values prepared by a student at a well-known university. He begins:

The faculty here misinterprets the traditional limitations upon the teaching of values. As a consequence, students receive little assistance or encouragement in their quest for personal values. . . . Some faculty members preclude all but the narrowest consideration of values when, for example, they have to expound what Byron or Hamilton "believed in." Others enlarge the treatment of values only by indulging in periodic allusions to their own so that students tend to be engulfed by and to accept the value systems of their instructors. What should happen is that students should find their value systems squarely challenged by competing systems. They should learn the means by which values can be examined and criticized. If the college is to equip students for their venture into the realm of values, the relationship between fact and value must be delineated, the clash of value systems must be considered, and the criticism of values must be encouraged.[4]

Just a short time ago I was discharging one of the endless duties of a university president—attending the annual dinner of a large business association. We had hardly been seated when one of the officers of the organization, a college-trained, public-spirited man, a leader in charitable and civic activity, turned to me and said: "You know, I lie awake night after night frightened by this thought: What is it all worth if there really isn't any afterlife?"

Have we omitted something crucial in American life? Is it just accidental that Nathan Pusey, from his platform of educational prominence as head of America's oldest institution of learning, has repeatedly called for the recognition of theology as an important source for the totality of truth and for its restoration to a respected place in the curriculum?[5]

I am aware of the philosophical and religious differences that divide us. But I am far more painfully aware of the failure of American higher education to make a positive contribution to the fight against communism. All of us are against it, of course. But what are we for? What values do we really hold? Isn't there, deep down, a real American consensus—a set of basic values that we hold sacred, that we are willing to fight and die for? In this, our hour of need, we Americans must bring to the surface and inject into the practicalities of life as it is today all the consequences of our convictions about the innate dignity of the human person and the right of each man to life, liberty, and the pursuit of happiness. Otherwise, our colleges and universities will go down in history as partially responsible for having lost something precious in their heritage, and we educators will stand guilty of short-changing our students. The alarming situation so accurately described by the prominent psychologist Dr. Ira Progoff must be changed:

> The essential occurrence that has made the modern world a predominantly secular organization is that the traditional beliefs and symbols of Western culture have been emptied of their inner content. During the past two centuries what had been felt to be the "spiritual" meaning of life has lost its ring of truth; consequently, modern man has been left without a frame of reference for his life. Only a vacuum of meaning has remained, and this vacuum is often filled by a shallow "scientism," a worship of science.[6]

It is my firm conviction that there is a basic American consensus and that our colleges and universities have the high privilege and opportunity of implanting the tenets of this consensus in the mind of every American student and of explaining them to every student from a foreign country who comes here to learn about America and the American way of life.

Some people take the position that neutrality on this matter is desirable. The difficulty with this is that neutrality is not possible. No matter how desirable one or another person of whatever religious heritage, or of none, might feel it to be, it simply cannot be. Our schools and colleges are not neutral on many of the crucial facets of life—on freedom vs. slavery, for example, or on knowledge vs. ignorance, or on character vs. the lack of it. And because educators make it clear that they believe in freedom and knowledge and character, sooner or later they must give those beliefs some kind of ultimate rootage, some kind of cosmic support. If they do not have the conviction that these beliefs are somehow in the essence of things, if they think all this is simply a relative matter, they will ultimately have no convictions at all.[7]

Now, if ever, we must assert our fundamental agreement on those values which give inner content to the traditional beliefs and symbols of Western culture, that undergird American democracy, give substance and meaning to life. They touch on all fields of human knowledge and must be taught by many disciplines. They should be taught, not negatively and apologetically, but boldly and positively. They should be taught with all the critical apparatus which modern scholarship can command, so that the students who come to us will leave us on commencement day with a set of values arrived at after serious, critical thought, and carry with them a conviction which results from thorough consideration of opposite opinions, a conviction which is a profoundly firm commitment to a cause—to the American way of life.

What then do I propose as a credo for American higher education?

In today's bitter struggle between the free world and the slave world—the free mind and the slave mind—American colleges and universities must unite in holding firm and in transmitting the essential values of our American way of life, values derived from the basic documents of American freedom. I trust, then, that as leaders of American higher education, we hold these truths:

"We believe in God.

We believe in the personal dignity of man.

We believe that man has natural rights which come from God and not from the State.

We are, therefore, opposed to all forms of dictatorship which are based on the philosophy that the "total man" (totalitarianism) belongs to the State.

We believe in the sanctity of the home—the basic unit of civilization.

We believe in the natural right of private property, but, likewise, that private property has its social obligations.

We believe that Labor has not only rights but obligations.

We believe that Capital has not only rights but obligations.

We are vigorously opposed to all forms of "racism"—persecution or intolerance because of race.

We believe that liberty is a sacred thing, but that law, which regulates liberty, is a sacred obligation.

We believe in inculcating all the essential liberties of American Democracy, and take open and frank issue with all brands of spurious "democracy."

We believe in the intense study of the tenets and tactics of those who would seek to destroy these essential liberties of American Democracy.

We believe that "academic freedom" should not be used as a pretext to advocate systems which destroy all freedom.

We believe that morality must regulate the personal, family, economic, political, and international life of men if civilization is to endure."[8]

These truths we believe and hold; and with these truths we shall weave "The Future Pattern of Higher Education."

*Delivered before the American Council on Education, Washington, D.C., October 6, 1961.*

## NOTES

1. Charles F. Donovan, "The Dean's Responsibility for Academic Excellence," in *The Jesuit Dean and Academic Excellence,* Proceedings of the Third National Institute for Deans held August 1961, Gonzaga University, Spokane, Wash. (New York, N.Y.: Jesuit Educational Association, 1961).

2. The Declaration of Independence.

3. Etienne Gilson, "The Breakdown in Morals and Christian Education," address, St. John Fisher College, Rochester, N.Y., 1960.

4. Henry Stolar, "What Happens to Student Values?" *Washington University Magazine,* June 1960, pp. 32–33 passim.

5. Nathan M. Pusey, "Religion's Role in Liberal Education," *Christian Century,* July 14, 1954, pp. 849–51; excerpts from baccalaureate address, *Time,* June 23, 1958, p. 54.

6. Ira Progoff, "Psychology as a Road to a Personal Philosophy," *Journal of Individual Psychology,* May 1961, p. 47.

7. Merrimon Cuninggim, "A Protestant View of Education," in *Philosophies of Education,* ed. Philip Phenix (New York: John Wiley & Sons, 1961), p. 68.

8. "Credo of Saint Louis University," printed in all bulletins of Saint Louis University, St. Louis, Mo.

# 2

# Responsibility of American
# Catholic Higher Education
# in Meeting National Needs

The preservation and development of Catholic higher education is based on the assumption that we have something
unique to offer for the benefit of American society. Past
decades give ample proof that our colleges and universities
have made a significant contribution to the educational,
cultural, and scientific growth of the United States. Our
responsibility today, therefore, in meeting national needs,
is to improve the quality of that specific kind of education
which is declared to be our unique objective. This paper is
intended to outline four mandates which are of special importance to us at this time in our history. These mandates
point to concrete positive steps which we must take if the
quality of our performance is to continue to grow.

First, Catholic higher education must plan and govern and

in some areas restrict its own growth lest it reach a point of proliferation where quality is seriously impaired. It is obvious that Catholic higher education can and should expand. What is to be avoided is unplanned growth, yet there seems to be rather alarming evidence that excessive proliferation is already in process, both in the case of colleges exclusively for religious, and in colleges intended largely for lay students.

In regard to colleges for religious, an NCEA Research Office report reveals that there are now 93 colleges for the education of Sisters, 49 of which have been founded within the last ten years, only three of the latter being regionally accredited. Statistics from 43 of these recently founded colleges show that the total full-time enrollment in all 43 was 2,094, with one-third (869) in the regionally accredited colleges. The total enrollment picture is as follows: fifteen colleges enroll 1 to 25 students; nineteen, 26 to 50 students; four, 51 to 75 students; one, 76 to 100 students; one, 101 to 200 students; three (the regionally accredited), over 200 students. The administration and teaching staff of these 43 colleges in 1961–62 totaled 437 full-time and 350 part-time persons. In all 43 colleges, 107 staff members hold a doctorate; 342, the Master's; 18, some professional degree; 118, the Bachelor's; 90, apparently no degree. The great cost to the religious communities that sponsor these colleges is underscored by the faculty-student ratio (excluding the three comparatively large, regionally accredited colleges) of one teacher for each 3.6 students. The study concludes: "the current great scarcity of well-qualified teaching staff at all levels of Catholic education makes it worth noting also that in these tiny colleges there are 358 persons holding advanced degrees, teaching only 2,032 students. This may be fully as important a consideration as the fact that these same students were being taught by 85 staff members who apparently had no degree at all.

What is our mandate in relationship to the education of religious? It helps no one to complain about this unhealthy proliferation of small, almost certainly weak institutions unless some positive solution to the obligation of various communities to educate our Sisters is proposed. The problem facing these congregations is a real one.

Religious commitment and quality in education can certainly be combined in one institution, but the presence of one of these factors does not necessarily presuppose the other. Since Religious communities must insure that both elements are present in the formation of their members they should look to cooperation with colleges and universities conducted by other groups in the Church to procure educational excellence. On their part large colleges and universities should stand ready to share their resources with communities in such a way that the legitimate aims of the communities are not jeopardized. Such aims do exist, and they are not co-extensive with general academic aims. The fact that smaller institutions open to lay students sometimes protest that they cannot "absorb" Sister students beyond a certain percentage points up that there is need for special planning for Sisters and that they constitute an unmistakably unique element in a student community, because of their consecration and specific apostolic commitment.

In themselves, neither smallness nor bigness can be appealed to as values in a school, apart from the total worth of an institution; nor can an institution be called weak merely because its entire student body consists of Sisters. Both the academic institution and the Religious community need to admit that Sisters require formation in view of their vocation; and they should be willing to plan imaginatively and generously for cooperation and sharing of resources. Neither group can use the other to advance its own aims, if this means anti-intellectualism on the one hand, or distrust of religious and spiritual objectives on the other. Neither group can engage in education which puts in hazard the standing of colleges and universities in the opinion of fair-minded secular persons qualified to judge; nor can either group afford to overlook the intrinsic importance of forming consecrated

Religious for an inestimable service in our society. These are the objectives which the Sister Formation Conference, a section of the College and University Department of this Association, is pursuing through its Educational Resources Committee, through NCEA programs, regional conferences, summer workshops, and publications.

There is equally alarming evidence of excessive, unplanned proliferation of new Catholic colleges for lay students. Since 1950, at least 54 new Catholic colleges for lay students have been established, 42 of them four-year institutions, and 12 junior colleges. Four additional senior colleges have announced that they will open in 1965. Considering the tremendous problem of adequate staffing for these new institutions, it is clear that they should have been established only for the very best and most cogent of reasons. Yet one frequently searches in vain for these compelling reasons. For example, it cannot be said that the new colleges are being established with an eye to geographical distribution in order to meet a need in areas that previously had no Catholic college. Twenty years ago there were thirteen states which did not have even one Catholic college. In the twenty intervening years up to the present, only 2 of the 54 new Catholic colleges have been established in states which had no previous Catholic college and only two other colleges have been opened up in areas remote from existing Catholic colleges. For the most part, these new colleges for lay students have been established in areas that are already reasonably well-supplied with Catholic higher education. In some cases, the new colleges are within easy walking distance of an existing institution which caters to the same clientele.

I share the sobering conviction of many that "one of the threats to the survival of all Catholic colleges of liberal arts is the alarming proliferation of new Catholic colleges at a time when the cost of operating these institutions has literally skyrocketed."[1] The initial cost of land and buildings for these new institutions is only a very minor part of the continuing financial investment required if a quality education worthy of our Catholic institutions is to be guaranteed. Most of this money must come from Catholic sources, and there has to be a limit somewhere. Today on all sides one hears a growing insistence on the part of Catholic philanthropists that the appeal for funds for Catholic higher education is doomed to fall on deaf ears unless evidence is forthcoming that the hierarchy, religious communities, and others responsible for the establishment of new Catholic institutions are guided by a carefully developed plan aimed at meeting the most critical needs of the Catholic population of this country, at meeting these critical needs with the maximum use of our limited resources in manpower and facilities, and with such ingenious methods of collaboration, coordination, and cooperation as have been developed by other segments of American higher education.

Secondly, if we are to maintain and enhance the quality of Catholic higher education, we must heed a second mandate, namely, that of providing faculties composed of dedicated, effective teachers and first-rate scholars in all of the academic curricula offered by the institution. In carrying out this mandate today, certain specific steps are essential:

In the case of our Religious teachers—priests, sisters, and brothers—we must provide for them the academic training and the opportunities for professional development that are comparable to the scholar-teachers in the nation's other private and public colleges and universities. These Religious men and women must be encouraged to devote themselves to fields which are studied for their own sake in order to promote the advancement and perfection of human knowledge. In her illuminating article last October, Sister Helen James John speaks cogently to this point:

> The biologist who has worked for years to grasp the scientific evidence of evolution; the historian who has come to a sympathetic understanding of the mind of Luther or Marx; the economist who day by day sees the grim facts of human necessity in the light of Christian responsibility; the teacher

of creative writing who can bring to fully formed expression the beauty and tragedy of a world charged with the grandeur of God:—these are masters whose vision the student can make his own, in whom he can see the reality of his own half-formed aspirations.[2]

This mandate affecting the religious members of our faculties demands greater attention than ever before to the two academic disciplines which constitute our specific difference from a curricular viewpoint: philosophy and theology. The insistent need for excellence in these departments in our Catholic institutions stems from

the need which every educated and intellectually self-aware human person has to be able to make certain basic, ultimate, and genuinely intellectual commitments about the ultimate truth of things, specifically about his own nature as a human person, about the goals and values which must ultimately determine his life and his attitudes toward it, about the nature of the world and the social order, and especially about the God who is (or is not) the one source Who gives meaning and intelligibility and purpose to all of reality.[3]

There is ample evidence to show that these needs of our students are often not being met by priests, sisters, or brothers in our departments of philosophy and theology, because they have not been given professional training comparable to that expected of their confreres in the secular disciplines. Fortunately, doctoral programs in both philosophy and theology already exist, and others are being established in some of our Catholic universities. The notion that the ordinary training common to all priests and religious is adequate for a college-level teaching of philosophy and theology must be abandoned forever. These subjects must be taught by men and women who have penetrated the intellectual core of Christian wisdom, and who can foster the mental formation of our students in such a way that these academic disciplines will contribute to their intellectual as well as to their moral and spiritual growth.

Another facet of the mandate relating to our faculties is that of strategic placement of our Religious teachers. Since it is obvious that Catholic colleges and universities neither can nor should be staffed entirely by religious, the placement of limited manpower resources within the institution is a matter of great importance. Efforts should be made even in the largest institutions to have at least one well-trained Religious scholar in each department, a heavy concentration of Religious in theology and philosophy, a substantial representation in the humanities, social sciences and education, and a smaller representation in the fields of natural sciences, business, engineering, and the professional curricula of Law, Dentistry, and Medicine. Strategic placement in these crucial areas or courses should produce the greatest impact on both the lay faculty and our student bodies. One well-trained Religious scholar in any given department, a colleague esteemed by his or her lay confreres in their area of academic competence, will be a better guarantee of the penetrating influence of Christian educational philosophy in that department than a large number of inadequately prepared Religious teachers.

The mandate for first-rate faculties also postulates a much wider and deeper involvement of our lay faculty and personnel. The shortage of competent and well-trained Religious in our colleges and universities makes this involvement not only a necessity, but an advantage as well. Although the participation of our lay confreres is rapidly growing in the instructional and research activities of our colleges and universities, several additional important fields of endeavor must be opened to them. Lay as well as Religious professors should be encouraged to take advantage of the doctoral programs in theology so that they may soon be in a position to make a major contribution to the academic life of our departments of theology, as some of them are already doing in philosophy. Likewise, lay men and women must be placed in strategic administrative positions where they, together with the total faculty, can have an influential voice in determining academic policy. Another neglected field where lay men and women can greatly alleviate our manpower problem is that of the co-curricular and extra-curricular life of the college. Lay personnel, professionally trained in counseling and student personnel work, should be given every opportunity to devote their talents to the student life programs on our campuses.

The third mandate requisite to the enhancement of the quality of our educational efforts requires greatly expanded educational opportunities for our students. This mandate, too, has a number of very practical implications.

Catholic colleges and universities must exert a more intelligent effort in seeking and admitting the "right" student. In other words, we must keep in step with the improved admissions procedures in superior colleges and universities. Admissions in our better colleges are being based more and more on the relation of the student's interests, abilities and aptitudes to the specific type and objectives of the individual institution itself. This makes more sense than the monolithic process of selecting students on their high school record and on one or more aptitude tests which are incapable of taking into consideration the kind of institution and curriculum involved. While we are all in institutions under Catholic auspices, it is obvious that each of our colleges and universities should be conscious of a clearly defined specific role to be played within the total spectrum of Catholic higher education. Having identified these specific objectives, we should proceed to recruit only those students who are interested in achieving these specific objectives, who are academically capable of the demands these specific objectives entail, and who are motivated to make the most of the opportunities offered. In the words of Alvin C. Eurich of the Fund for the Advancement of Education, the Admissions Officer today must "look both to the past and to the future, rather than being concerned with a snapshot judgment of the present. He must perceive the pattern of each individual's growth in his past education, and he must understand the educational program of his own institution intimately enough to see how the student's record and achievement profile can interlock with the institution's offerings."[4]

Our colleges and universities must provide increased financial assistance in the form of scholarships, grants-in-aid, and loans to the qualified needy student. Unlike past practice in too many Catholic colleges, this financial assistance must be funded, not merely written off. This means that a financial aid program for students must be devised consonant both with the institution's educational objectives and its financial potential. Financial-Aid Officers must be perceptive enough to face the peculiar situation of each applicant, not with an unvarying routine or formula, but with individualized treatment. The need analysis of the College Scholarship Service should be used as a helpful guide, not as a rigid scientific law. Professor Frederick Rudolph of Williams College, addressing the first colloquium on financial aid to the College Scholarship Service said, "Higher education in the United States has always been untidy; it will probably never be an orderly house. Surely, however, it has now reached a point where it can take a responsible inventory of its resources for student aid, make some effort to understand their historical and philosophical foundations and tendencies, and undertake a new and bold adventure in subsidies for wisdom, investments in democracy."[5]

Our faculties must exert greater effort and ingenuity in discharging our obligation to the most capable students in our institutions. What is each of us doing in an organized, adequately financed program to motivate highly talented students to achieve their potential for excellence? Much can be learned from the wide variety of successful plans now in operation in some of our Catholic colleges and universities. Though it is impossible to mention them all, let me list just a few which can be considered significantly representative: Boston College, San Francisco College for Women, Mundelein College (Chicago), Xavier University (Cincinnati), Fordham University, St. Michael's College (Vermont), University of Santa

Clara, Providence College, Notre Dame, and Saint Louis University. One evidence of the effectiveness of this type of program in these institutions is the large number of graduate fellowships and assistantships, the prizes, and other awards which the talented students in these programs are receiving annually.

In the light of the revolutionary developments in the liturgical life of the Christian, our students today have a right to demand that Catholic colleges and universities re-assess the conduct of religious activities on our campus, those activities which presumably are part and parcel of our unique system of higher education, which professedly promote the Christian life and holiness of our students, and which specifically contribute to their moral, religious, and spiritual formation. Religious activities common to all institutions—the Mass, the sacraments, prayer, retreats and sodalities—should be centrally presided over by a trained chaplain or director of religious activities, assisted by a faculty committee charged with the responsibility of planning and supervising an integrated religious program for the entire academic year. The officer in charge of the religious activities should have a status and a stature in harmony with the high place this facet of student life holds among the goals of the institution. Such status and stature require a suitable staff, physical facilities, and a budget adequate for a full-blown religious program, including the attendance of both students and faculty at appropriate conventions, the inclusion of religious topics in institutional lecture series, public relations, and intra-institutional communications.

Much greater attention must also be given to the non-religious life of the student outside the classroom. Disillusioning experience has shown time and again that we cannot take it for granted that the principles taught in our classrooms will automatically be adopted by students outside the classroom. Father Walsh, President of Boston College, has written that there is "a growing body of evidence" which indicates that students themselves are just as likely to set the ethos of a campus as they are to adopt an institution-sponsored ethos, and that they are more apt to take their values from each other than from their professors and the administration. Catholic colleges and universities are well aware of the educational significance of religious activities on campus; they must be equally aware of the educational significance of non-religious activities. It should be the purpose of the non-religious program to develop students who may be trusted to conduct themselves among their peers with adequate Christian wisdom not only as students, but also through life as citizens in a free society. Most important are those extra-class activities which involve the students themselves in the responsibilities which accompany the making of laws and the exercise of delegated authority. The full benefit of the non-religious activities program can be achieved only if it is structured to encourage the growth of personal and group responsibility. The total campus atmosphere should be such as to provide opportunity for the development of leadership qualities in the student. Clear concept with respect to the nature, necessity, and limits of authority can be taught and learned in the disciplines of philosophy and theology. But they will be worthless to our students if we, the responsible agents who exercise authority within our own institutions, do not do so with deep respect for the dignity, rights, freedoms, and degree of maturity which the individual student possesses.

The fourth and final mandate for the enhancement of quality in our institutions of higher learning is the demand for stabilized financial support. Though this critical problem of financing has a multitude of facets, my observations regarding many Catholic colleges and universities has convinced me of four key requirements:

We must take a realistic position in respect to what we charge for our educational services. In our noble obsession down through the years to keep tuition at the very minimum, we blinded ourselves to the galloping imbalance between expenditures and income. With each new building, with each new faculty member, with each new student, our expenditures for general educational operations continue to climb. In spite of the fierce competitive position in which many of us may find ourselves in regard to tax-supported institutions, we must continue to increase our tuition charges. At the same time we must educate our students and parents to their responsibility for bearing a fair share of the rapidly-growing costs of higher education. If we are offering quality education, we are justified in tuition rates comparable to those in quality secular private colleges and universities. We are not being honest with our students if we allow the disproportion between tuition and the actual costs of instruction to undermine our traditions of educational excellence.

In addition to a substantial base of tuition support, we must establish in all our institutions a well-organized development program. No Catholic college can be satisfied that its future is secure until it has in operation a program of continuing voluntary support from corporations, foundations, individuals, alumni, parents, and students. Such support from multiple sources will be needed over and above the financial assistance from the federal government which hopefully will also increase in years ahead. Religious as well as lay staff must be trained and dedicated to this recognized and respectable area of college and university life. To quote Father Stanford again:[6]

> Tackle first those tasks which are closest at hand—alumni annual giving, parent and student efforts. Then there are the activities where trustees and associate board members must help, solicitations from business and industrial corporations and the like. Finally, there are the longer-range programs which deal with special gifts, wills, bequests and the like. These require careful preparation and patient cultivation on the part of many selected individuals.

Fifteen years of educational fund raising has convinced me that there are at least three essential ingredients, one or more of which is too often missing in the typical support program of our institutions: continuity, investment in manpower and money, and the help of volunteers. A program for support that operates in fits and starts due to changing institutional leadership is doomed to failure. Again, many development programs fail because those responsible do not have sufficient faith in their efforts to make the necessary prerequisite investment for successful results. There is no other way: it costs money to raise money. Continuity of leadership together with willingness to invest still demands the invaluable advice and aid of lay volunteers. And laymen can advise and act with wisdom and power only if they are allowed to acquire an intimate knowledge of the college or university for which they are working. Better not to have an advisory board at all than to keep vital information to ourselves.

Another guarantee of financial stability should be the approach we take towards the construction and maintenance of our physical facilities. Today there is no justification whatever for the erection of new buildings that are costly monuments, architect's dreams, yet ill-fitted to our total financial potential, to modern teaching techniques, and to economical maintenance and repair. It has been said, and so rightly, that master planning can be the best money higher education spends; and in planning, the watchword is flexibility—the optimum utilization of space and architectural design to accomplish this end. As Harold B. Gores of the Educational Facilities Laboratories aptly remarks in his "Bricks and Mortarboards": "A college or university is people, ideas, and a place—and in that order. A college or university aspiring to completeness in all things will somehow find a way to cast up a physical environment that supports and sustains its mission."[7]

Finally, financial stability for Catholic higher education must be fostered by ceaseless ingenious efforts to combine our resources both with other Catholic institutions and with secular colleges and universities. Inter-institutional cooperation is the emerging concept in American higher education. In non-

Catholic circles it is proving itself capable of producing academic and cultural stimulation to the whole higher educational program. While thus far we Catholics are not conspicuous for leadership in this movement, at least there are many encouraging evidences of awareness of the potential and of courage to initiate one form or another of pooling of resources. Our more complex universities can strengthen themselves mightily in the graduate and professional fields by investigating seriously the promising possibilities of such arrangements as have been announced in Washington, D.C. where American, Catholic, Georgetown, George Washington and Howard Universities have formed the "Joint Graduate Consortium of Washington Universities" by agreeing to pool their facilities for graduate students under one director. Beginning next September, a graduate student enrolled at any one of these five universities will be able to take one or more courses at any of the other four universities. The degree will be awarded by the university in which he originally enrolled. A similar agreement in the field of graduate nursing has been achieved by Washington and Saint Louis Universities and we are currently exploring several other graduate academic programs in relation to which this agreement will be extended. Undergraduate education in all our colleges and universities may well be strengthened without additional financial burden, even possibly with great savings, if more of us are willing to shake off the shackles of isolationism as has been done, for example, in the St. Thomas-St. Catherine's-Macalester-Hamline program in the Twin Cities area, which offers jointly an area-studies curriculum which previously was out of reach for any one of the four institutions. Fortunately, sound programs in which colleges and universities primarily for lay students are coordinating their faculties and facilities with programs for the education of religious teachers are multiplying. Before starting a new tiny college, Religious superiors should certainly investigate the "Sister Formation" programs now in progress, for example, at institutions in Milwaukee, Chicago, Seattle and St. Louis.

To summarize: the responsibility of Catholic colleges and universities in meeting national needs today will be carried out with distinction only if we enhance the quality of their achievement of our unique objectives. Today this is possible only if, in expanding our services, we: 1) avoid unsound proliferation; 2) enhance the professional competence of our faculties both religious and lay; 3) enrich the educational opportunities of our students; and 4) stabilize our financial support. These four mandates should press heavily on each one of our institutions and on those of us who are responsible for their administration. I cannot conclude, however, without repeating what was said earlier. These four mandates imply a fifth which demands more than any one or any small group of us can bring to realization: an objective, carefully prepared, flexible blueprint for the general development of Catholic higher education in this country. Obviously, this blueprint, if it did exist, should not be imposed by an authority within or outside our own colleges and universities. Ideally, it should be the result of our own voluntary efforts to accomplish what is obviously needed. Practically, it may be forced on us by the decision of those on whom all of us directly or indirectly depend—the benefactors, mostly Catholic, whose contributions are essential to our future growth and development. Before they move farther towards a unified refusal to support unplanned Catholic higher education, I would urge that we do what is overdue at once.

*Delivered before the National Catholic Education Association at its 61st annual convention, 1964.*

### NOTES

1. Edward V. Stanford, O.S.A., Lessons Learned from Visiting Colleges." Speech delivered at Winter meeting, Eastern Regional Unit,

National Catholic Educational Association, February 22, 1964, Villanova University.

2. Sister Helen James John, "Toward the Open College," *Commonweal*, October 4, 1963.

3. "The Role of Philosophy and Theology as Academic Disciplines and the Integration with the Moral, Religious, and Spiritual Life of the Jesuit College Student." Workshop of the Jesuit Educational Association, Loyola in Los Angeles, August 1962. Selected papers from this Workshop appear in J. Barry McGannon, ed., *Christian Wisdom and Christian Formation* (New York: Sheed and Ward, 1963).

4. Alvin C. Eurich, "College Admissions in the 21st Century," *College Board Review*, Fall 1962.

5. Frederick Rudolph, "Myths and Realities of Student Aid." *College Board Review*, Fall 1962.

6. Edward V. Stanford, O.S.A. *Catholic Educational Review*, 1961.

7. Harold B. Gores, "Bricks and Mortarboards." Conference on Higher Education, 1963.

# 3

# Why the Catholic College?

Perhaps one of the most perplexing questions that the Catholic educator must ask himself, in this rapidly changing world of education, is, Why Catholic higher education?

The temptation is almost overpowering to answer that we exist because we make up 30% of the total or national effort. This is as irrelevant an argument as the one offered by parents of parochial school children who ask their neighbors, "What if all of *our* children went to *your* school?"

It would seem to me equally fallacious to say that the Catholic college faculty, perhaps because it is not as well paid as other private and state university faculty, is more dedicated.

To say that Catholic universities and colleges have adequate facilities, that they offer a variety of comparable degree pro-

grams and subjects, are equally fallacious arguments for the
rationale of the Catholic college.

Is it that we have committed so many Religious to the field
of education or that we have invested so much money in brick
and mortar that we cannot pull out? None of these reasons
provides the *prima facie* rationale for Catholic higher education.

Instead, let us cut through this haze of irrelevance and
come to grips with the truth. The truth is that the product of
Catholic higher education is or should be unique. If at any
time we fail to identify the *uniqueness* of this product, we
have then denied the rationale of Catholic higher education.

It is unfortunate that some Catholic educators seem to
suffer from the haunting doubt that their product has a
uniqueness, and would rather resort to the old ecclesiastical
bromides about Johnny's obligation to go to a Catholic school.

As an aside, may I interject this idea about all Catholic
education. If we are not capable of identifying any unique
quality in our graduates, whether it be on the university or
the parochial school level, then I think we have an obligation
to those who have given the trust to us as educators, to re-
evaluate our curriculum, and, if need be, the whole educational environment of our institution.

If we as Catholic educators cannot transmit an additional
quality to our graduates beyond the accumulation of knowledge, then we should give up our mandate as Catholic educators. It is not enough that Johnny should learn to read and
write or become a biophysicist in an institution which is different solely because it is supported by Catholic dollars.

What are some valid arguments for the Catholic college?

The first reason for the existence of the Catholic college
and the importance of attendance by Catholics at such institutions should be established in the broader context of higher
education, especially that under private auspices. We should
expect that, among other motivating factors, students will
select a Catholic college or university for the same reasons

they select other colleges and universities. Obviously, many students choose a particular college because of geographical proximity or other superficial reasons. However, I am referring to two special reasons why a student selects a college. First, the specific college or university has achieved recognized academic excellence in undergraduate instruction, or at least acknowledged superiority in certain programs. Or, secondly, a specific program desired by the prospective student and offered by the college is generally not offered in other schools. These are the two reasons why we should expect students to look at a specific college—public, private, or Catholic.

Over and above these reasons which we share with other segments of private higher education, we still must establish a third important reason, which is the theme of my remarks today.

Again, may I restate my thesis: a) the graduate of a Catholic college is or should be unique, and, b) because he is unique, he is an asset to society.

Up to this point I could be accused of begging the question, of hiding the bird in the bush and then discovering my find. You might even accuse me of all sorts of Jesuitical trickery in having suggested that, if Catholic higher education is not unique, then we should get out; that we cannot turn back (as all of us have been in this game too long to know how to do anything else); that we must find out why it is unique, in order that we may be saved the embarrassment of having to turn back. This was not my intent.

Let us examine the first question: Are the graduates of Catholic colleges unique?

Obviously, it would be foolhardy to try to generalize about the quality of the education received by the graduates of all of the 295 Catholic colleges and universities in the United States. But, conceding that there are possibly twenty or twenty-five universities in the country which excell any Catholic institution in the general quality of their undergraduate academic program, I would argue that considering the remain-

ing spectrum of higher education, one could identify Catholic
colleges and universities that are the acknowledged peer of
secular institutions in the quality of their faculties, the adequacy of their libraries, laboratories and other physical facilities, and in the academic ability and motivation of their student body. But the most we can claim is that we share the
essential ingredients of a good college education with other
institutions. We cannot claim any of the academic ingredients
as uniquely ours any more than we can claim that we have
cornered the market by devising unique methodologies to develop the intellect, the will, the physical or the emotional
facets of man's nature.

Nor can we argue that Catholic higher education is alone in
its profound dedication to the liberal arts, to an education
that transcends the accumulation of information or the amassing of knowledge. Many secular institutions would endorse
and are attempting to realize in their students the aim of
liberal education as described by the Secretary-General of the
Guggenheim Memorial Foundation, Gordon H. Ray: "The
aim of liberal education, then, is not primarily the amassing
of a large amount of factual information. Rather it is the enlargement of mental capacity that can come through the
process of *acquiring, ordering,* and *reflecting* upon such information."

What, then, is the uniqueness of Catholic college education?
As part of the total complex of higher education, the Catholic
college, in common with all colleges worthy of the name, is
formally dedicated to truth as such; that is, to intellectual
knowledge, to its extension and development, to its preservation and communication. The college's obligation to truth is
its obligation to society. Within the total complex of higher
education, the college is specifically dedicated to the development of mature human beings. Though the college is established by a social commitment as an institution for the development of human beings, once so established, it must be
governed, in all its activities, by the truth about human

nature, and *this* does not depend upon a social decision or consensus.

And here we enter into the truly unique character of Catholic college education. Our dedication to truth is guided by what we know about human nature from both natural and supernatural sources. Our education is based on the *Catholic* idea of human nature and the *Catholic* ideal of human development. For us, the humanistic tradition, philosophy, and theology all come to the same conclusion: the highest and the noblest level of man's life is his ability to know and to love. Through the supreme liberality of Divine Love, God has set as the final term of man's growth and development the complete fulfillment of that hunger and thirst for reality which displays itself in knowing and loving. This term is, however, a trans-terrestrial good; yet not unrelated to present living, for it is precisely the goal of each human life as it is lived here. From the standpoint of the Catholic college, the growth of human beings must be continuously a growth towards the supreme fulfillment, the vision of Truth itself. Moreover, this term—though it is supernatural—is not unnatural and, indeed, presupposes nature, and, ideally, the full development of nature. In the Catholic view, a college education must include the development and perfecting of the total human being. Hence no education is complete unless it includes the intellectual, moral, religious and spiritual formation of the student. All courses, all activities, all personnel must contribute, according to their own natures, to this overall and essential objective. Particularly must the academic disciplines of philosophy and theology, which are the core of Christian wisdom, foster the total formation of the college student.[1]

That this total formation in Christian wisdom is achieved in each Catholic college graduate would be, of course, an indefensible claim. What is certain, however, is that the objective of a complete and total Christian synthesis in the collegiate education of a young man or woman cannot take place except in an atmosphere which can be created solely in a Catholic college. Only in a climate pervaded with Christ-centered attitudes, commitments and values can an undergraduate receive the unique, distinctive kind of education described by Cardinal Newman:

> I wish the intellect to range with the utmost freedom, and religion to enjoy an equal freedom, but what I am stipulating for is, that they should be found in one and the same place, and exemplified in the same person . . . It will not satisfy me, if religion is here, and science, there, and young men converse with science all day, and lodge with religion in the evening . . . I want the same roof to contain both the intellectual and moral disciplines.[2]

Moreover, I would argue that Catholic college education is unique, not only because wholehearted commitment to the objectives of education in Christian wisdom is *possible* in a Catholic institution, but also because such commitment is *impossible* in any other kind of college or university. For example, such total commitment cannot be obtained nor such a Christian-wisdom climate of learning created by a Newman Center at a secular university. Please do not misunderstand this statement. I am a member of the Board of the National Newman Foundation; I have deep convictions about the necessity and importance of this apostolate; but I am also aware of the severe handicaps with which this apostolate must contend. Therefore, I would agree enthusiastically with this statement from a recent article in *America:*

> There is a compelling need for instruction not offered in high schools or Newman Centers. This includes courses in philosophy (especially in ethics and natural theology, and in the arts, history and literature, taught on advanced levels from a Catholic viewpoint. Such instruction cannot be had, I agree, unless the student attends a Catholic college. But, then, unless a lack of money prevents him, why shouldn't he?

> As a matter of fact, the intricate network of Catholic colleges in America is being recognized as the last outpost of

truly liberal education—which paradoxically, is even more
important in this era of specialization than ever it was
before.[3]

This would be the appropriate juncture to consider a criticism voiced at times against Catholic colleges, namely, that
the unique environment of which I have been speaking is
over-protective, over-concerned with providing safety from
sin. I am satisfied that whatever validity this criticism may
have had in the past in respect to some of our Catholic colleges, this is a weakness which is fast disappearing. We are
not conducting our colleges and universities for future occu-
pants of Catholic ghettos but for potential Catholic leaders in
a pluralistic world. Virtue can only be acquired when the environment is free enough to test the individual's free will.
Besides giving the student the opportunity of disciplining the
will and the intellect, of acquiring and ordering information
on the undergraduate level, the Catholic college affords him
the environment in which he can project proper values and
attitudes. As he reflects on his acquired and ordered knowledge as a maturing and responsible adult, he can test the focal
point of all his efforts, remembering that wisdom is the ordering of all things to one end, a moral end.

And this consideration leads logically to the second argument I have posited for a Catholic college, namely, that the
graduate of a Catholic college is an asset to the Christian
community and to our total pluralistic society. It seems to me
that American life today is desperately in need of a wholesale
injection of the kind of mature and wise citizens which the
Catholic college is uniquely equipped to produce. We all
know the multiple factors which have created a United States,
in fact a world, which is unprecedented, unpredictable, and
totally dominated by science and materialism. The most disrupting factor of all, of course, has been the explosion of
human knowledge itself. With techniques and instrumentali-
ties never before available, the scientist and the technologist

are adding to the sum total of human knowledge with such volume and rapidity that what used to require years of intellectual achievement is now reduced to a matter of minutes. For the first time in history it would seem that our output of scientific knowledge is, at least for the moment, too great for human beings to be able to absorb and harness for useful, humanitarian purposes.

What kind of an education does a college graduate today need not merely to cope with this frightening prospect but to make a substantial positive contribution to a society that has rightly been described as seriously sick? The college graduate needs two basic qualities if he is to live a meaningful, constructive life in today's world. First, his education must have given him adaptability. In today's complex economy specialized skills are as important as ever, but the specialties do not stay put as long as they used to. Over 70 per cent of the skilled trades needed in American manufacturing in the year 1900 do not exist today. And the same dynamic change is going on in the skills needed in professional fields. Most of the techniques and processes now considered essential in engineering and business and law and in the health fields will become obsolete long before the year 2000, yet this is a period shorter than the span of the average man's productive lifetime.

More than ever before, therefore, the best college education is the one that develops a young man or woman into what is more important than being a specialist. Today's college graduate must above all else have learned how to learn. This means that he must be able to understand what he reads, to think for himself, to express his thoughts clearly, to grasp the basic realities of his natural and human environment. This mature adaptability is the first requisite for true success in a changing society; it is a quality which any strong liberal arts college can develop.

But it is clear that adaptability to change is not sufficient guarantee of a fruitful life, and it is my contention that coupled with adaptability must be a second quality, one which only a Catholic college can develop in its entirety—the stability which alone gives meaning to life. As the Rockefeller Brothers study indicated:

> What most people, young or old, want is not merely security or comfort or luxury—although they are glad enough to have these. They want meaning in their lives. If their era and their culture and their leaders do not or cannot offer them great meanings, great objectives, great convictions, they will settle for shallow and trivial meanings.[4]

The stability that can support great meanings in life must be grounded in the religious and ethical values of life. The Catholic college recognizes that the development of an individual's potentialities must occur in the context of such religious and ethical values. Unlike the situation that is common elsewhere, education in a Catholic college is not just a mechanical process of communication of certain skills and information. It springs from our most deeply rooted convictions; it is carried on by teachers and students infused with the eternal values on which the system is built. This is the unique argument for Catholic education urged twenty years ago by Jacques Maritain in his *Education at the Crossroads:*[5] "The essence of education does not consist in adapting a potential citizen to the conditions and interactions of social life, but first in making a man, and by this very fact in preparing a citizen." Only the Catholic college can produce the individual with *both* essential qualities to be an asset in today's society: the adaptability to meet the demands of a dynamic revolution in human knowledge, and the stability to remain unperturbed in adherence to the God-given principles that alone give meaning to human existence.

This, then, is my answer to the question: "Why a Catholic College?" If the answer is true that only the Catholic college can produce the graduate who is unique in his acquisition of Christian wisdom and hence a unique asset to society, what are the reasons that would prevent our young people from seeking the advantages of a Catholic college education? On the assumption I made at the beginning of my remarks that a Catholic college can provide the academic program desired at an equally high level of quality, I believe that you would agree with me that by all odds the greatest obstacle is that of meeting the costs of financing a young man or woman through a Catholic college or university. For this reason, I want to conclude with some practical considerations that I hope will be of assistance to you high school principals and counselors who are faced daily with the problem of showing parents and students how they may achieve the reality of a Catholic college education in their own case.

Catholic education is at the crossroads with all private education in this matter of holding down tuition costs while maintaining the high academic standards that private universities and colleges—and their patrons—have come to expect.

We are fortunately in a new era, where businesses, foundations, and the government have become cognizant of our contribution to American society. They are reciprocating with assistance, not only to help us maintain our exceptionally high academic quality, but also to allow us to keep educational costs at a level at which qualified students may find it possible to benefit by attending our Catholic universities and colleges.

It is no secret that college is expensive. Nevertheless, many families are finding ways to meet the rising costs of sending a boy or girl to college. Unfortunately, the first impulse of many parents is to settle for the least expensive school that they can find—though few people would dream of making any other major purchase, such as a house or a car, so imprudently. Education is an investment. Catholic education is also an investment, materially and spiritually.

Let us briefly examine the realities of financing a college education. Today, sizable scholarship funds are becoming available to the academically talented and needy student, through expanded scholarship programs. In addition, many scholarship programs are open to prospective Catholic college students through federal and state agencies, business and service clubs, as well as through scholarship programs, such as the National Merit program.

In order to supplement the existing scholarship programs, many Catholic universities and colleges have established grant-in-aid programs that are designed to assist the many deserving scholarship applicants who fail to win a four-year scholarship. In the case of Saint Louis University, for example, in the last two years we have doubled the number of scholarships available to high school seniors.

A generally accepted thesis that is shared by many educators is that the student should help contribute financially towards his education. The student job-placement office has become an integral part of the student service program of most Catholic universities and colleges. It is often very feasible, and not detrimental, for a student to be employed ten to fifteen hours a week while in attendance at college. It has been our experience that there are more jobs available than requests from needy students.

In addition to the above assistance, generally administered by the respective school, is the establishment of various tuition and housing budget plans. As an example, we at Saint Louis University have developed two such programs that make it possible for the parents and student to meet their financial obligations. Under one program, tuition fees are paid on a monthly basis throughout the four-year period until the student graduates. This program is maintained without charging interest, though there is a small service charge for administering the program.

Comparatively new financial avenues open to the prospective college student are the various federal, state and commercial loan programs. The tremendous expansion of loan programs is due to a growing conviction about the soundness of the philosophy expressed in a report by the President's Committee on Education Beyond the High School: "Too little recognition has been given to education as an investment for the individual—as important and worthy of credit as machinery and equipment if he were to start in business. It is highly desirable that the use of loans for college education be popularized."[6]

The National Defense Education Act makes it possible for a student to borrow up to five thousand dollars, interest free, until one year after graduation. At that time, the student has an additional ten years to repay the loan at the rate of three per cent a year.

These and similar programs, particularly if several of them are utilized by the capable but needy student, make it possible for hundreds of our Catholic youth to go to a Catholic college. I am confident that the governmental scholarship and loans programs will be substantially expanded in either the present or the next session of Congress. It is essential, therefore, that all of us, particularly those who are responsible for counseling at the high school level, should be fully aware of the vast variety of financial aids which are available so that Catholic parents and students may be dissuaded from reaching a quick, unsubstantiated decision that a Catholic college education is out of the question for them

If Catholic education alone can produce that unique kind of Christian citizen that is so desperately needed in society today, then it is incumbent on us as Catholic educators to labor unceasingly for its maximum efficacy. Let it be our unwavering determination that, if possible, no obstacle, financial or otherwise, shall prevent a talented young boy or girl from sharing in the glorious opportunity of a Catholic college education.

*Delivered before a convocation at Gonzaga University, Spokane, 1964.*

## NOTES

1. The observations on the uniqueness of Catholic college education are based on the discussions in the Workshops of the Jesuit Educational

Association, Loyola University, Los Angeles, August 1962. Selected papers from this Workshop appear in J. Barry McGannon, ed., *Christian Wisdom and Christian Formation* (New York: Sheed and Ward, 1963).

2. John Cardinal Newman, "Intellect, the Instrument of Religious Training," *Sermons Preached on Various Occasions.*

3. Gerald B. Fugate, "Where Are You Going?" *America,* May 16, 1964, pp. 674–5.

4. "The Pursuit of Excellence," *Rockefeller Brothers Fund Report,* p. 48.

5. Jacques Maritain, *Education at the Crossroads* (New Haven: Yale University Press, 1943).

6. *Second Report to the President by the President's Committee on Education Beyond the High School* (U.S. Government Printing Office, July 1957).

# 4

# The University and the Inmost Life of Man

At this celebration of the 125th anniversary of the founding of Notre Dame there could hardly be a more appropriate theme than the one you have chosen: "The University in a Developing World Society," for Notre Dame can look back to her past role in such development with a pride exceeded only by confidence in the role which the future will give to her. May I, then, take this opportunity to congratulate the whole Notre Dame community on this celebration and on the theme which it has chosen.

The theme itself is so comprehensive, however, and the responsibilities of a university so multiple now and in the future that one can hardly hope to deal with them in their entirety. Four such responsibilities have been singled out for discussion in this academic symposium, and so before turning to an extended treatment of my particular subject, the responsibility of the university to what I shall call the inmost life of man. I would like briefly to situate it in relationship to those other three facets of this total responsibility.

First, it is almost a cliché to say that we are all inextricably involved in the turmoil and the promise of a developing world society. (Of course, a cliché is such in part because it is so obviously true.) Such a society has come into being and is in the process of development in large measure because of an almost exponential extension and refinement of knowledge over the past few centuries. To see how true this is in an academic context, we have only to look at the research journals ranged over ever-increasing lengths of library shelves, or we need only count up the scholarly publications too numerous in any one field to be dealt with other than in abstracts which themselves threaten to engulf the serious student. Knowing we shall fail, we can only try to keep up with the never-ending round of conventions, congresses and conferences, devoted to serious consideration of any one or more of hundreds of scholarly fields. And such progression gives little or no sign of any abatement in the future other than in the utter madness of an atomic holocaust carried out by the powers which have most benefitted from this knowledge explosion. To this extension and refinement of knowledge as a key element in a developing world society the university quite rightly addresses itself, and it takes on a responsibility commensurate with its high calling.

But, secondly, the university takes on such a responsibility in a particular context different from that of a pure research institute or a technical governmental bureau. It is the context of a community, a shared community of scholars and students, engaged ideally, however far short we fall in practice, in a common interactive venture. To some of the implications of community I shall come later in this paper. For the moment, and for every moment in the life of the university, it is important to recall that if this is indeed such a community of persons, then the university has to be concerned, beyond simple knowledge, with the personal needs of its members, and especially of its students as they engage in their last formal preparation for mature roles in such a rapidly changing society as ours. This, the specific responsibility to the needs of its students, is the second area of discussion in the present symposium.

Thirdly, neither the expansion and refinement of knowledge nor the personal needs of the newer members of the academic community are situated in a vacuum. They do not exist in a solipsistic or even a privatistic world. They are ineluctably situated within the context of a world of political and social forms. Those forms are concurrently shaped by ourselves while they in turn shape us. For our own sakes and for a future developing world society, the university must be concerned with a critical appraisal of, and an imaginative program for, such forms and institutions. It must concern itself with the knowledge and intelligent compassion which its students will, as fully participating citizens, bring to their shaping of the political and social institutions of tomorrow. The university cannot help being, directly and indirectly, a major social institution, and as such it will have, say yea or say no, an influence on the politics of our world.

It is in the context of these three university engagements in a developing world that I now turn to what may be, perhaps, an even more fundamental responsibility of the university, and one even more difficult of fulfillment: What is the responsibility of the university to the inmost life of man?

Let me describe rather than define what is meant by this term, the inmost life of man. When we have concerned ourselves as deeply as possible with the expansion of knowledge, with the needs of the students, and with the political and social order of the future, when we have implemented those concerns to the best of our ability, an ultimate "why?" still remains. This "why" sums up, all too poignantly at times, the need felt by every society, every age, every culture, and by every man for answers to ultimate questions. To the problem of the university's involvement in such questions I wish to address myself. This is the problem of how the university copes with, comes to terms with, engages itself in, a facet of reality with which it seems regularly to have found itself acutely uncomfortable.

Like it or not, praise it or decry it, the university cannot ignore or wish away the fact that man does ask ultimate questions, does have metaphysical problems, does structure his most basic anxieties and his most radical hopes, his deepest sorrows and his almost inexpressible joys into meaningful systems of belief and practice, whether these beliefs and practices be specifically religious or not. Does the university have any obligation to assist man in this never-ending search for an over-arching principle of unity, for the nature of transcendence, for the ultimate purpose of being, for the root source of the total "otherness" which he all too often experiences? Should the university enter into the area of the images and symbols and values by which man has always sought to express and cope with his deepest interior experiences?

My answer to this most serious of questions is that the university has no choice but to do so. The university in our present developing world society *does* have a responsibility to assist man in his stirring toward those spiritual, religious, metaphysical, ultimate, call them what you will, ideals and aspirations. They are not only man's most intimate glory and most intimate cross; they also play so significant a role in giving richness and power and depth to all the facets of what we call the processes of civilization and culture.

I know, of course, that in more recent times the university has been highly reluctant to venture outside the realm of almost purely intellectual development as its overriding primary task. And I—as all of us—must respect this single-minded concern, born out of an utterly sincere desire to develop the mind of modern man to its fullest, a fullness which always exceeds our ability to provide for it. Yet, I repeat that this is now not enough. It is increasingly borne in upon the thoughtful observer that for all the expansion of knowledge, for all the concern for the immediate material wants of man, for all the hopes put in the perfecting of a just political and social system, there is still an ever-growing feeling that present-day man is cut adrift, without ultimate meaning and without guiding purpose for his life.

I maintain that this drift will continue unless the university enters into the situation. More importantly, I maintain that in many instances only the university, the university alone, can do something about it. The university is the only modern instrumentality which will be able to cope with this malaise of emptiness, this seemingly hollow and vacuous re-echo of the question, "Why?".

These are startling statements, I know, and perhaps I ought briefly to make clear what, in playing such a role, the university is and is *not*. I am not suggesting that the university is or should be a surrogate church, nor do I at all think that knowledge is a substitute for religious faith. Nor is the university to be a substitute Maecenas, providing redemption or at least ultimate meaning through the higher forms of artistic endeavor. So far I am simply saying that there is no other institution realistically available to many men to help them effectively in this most basic of queries. Not the family, nor the state, nor any economic organization, nor any ideology, not even the church in the sense of any particular religious body. Whether any one of the foregoing ought to be available, whether any one of them is in itself a better instrumentality, whether man ought to choose one of them, is not the question here and now. Here and now, it seems to me, only the university can begin—and I say *begin* advisedly—can begin to fill this void.

Why is this so? As over the last several centuries, little by little, man's view of nature and man's view of his own nature have changed, as man became "modern man," he has been emancipating himself, albeit often unknowingly, from ancient signposts and anchor holds of custom and tradition. Much of the Western world lives today amid the personal consequences of emancipation from established authority, and if we are to believe the signs of the times, such a Western world is to be the paradigm for other lands and other peoples. In the course of this emancipation and in the course of the rationalization of so much of our lives, the old signposts of a fixed and traditional order, the comforting, or at least solid, authority of unchanging ecclesiastical or political orders, the cake of custom, the support of discipline, the surety of social status, the certainty of usage, all have progressively been left behind.

The guides to which a man could turn in his questioning have so often lost existence or, perhaps more often, credibility. But the questions remain. What is good? What is true? Who am I? What am I doing here? Why am I at all? And the questions are often an oblique way of affirming that there is a mystery about the human person and his destiny, that there is "something about our being here which is unsettled and unfinished."

If such is the nature of man (if one may be permitted to use that somewhat unfashionable phrase), or if such is at any rate his existential condition, if he continues to ask such questions, why should it be the university to which he turns, indeed in many cases, must turn for an answer? First, so many of the other repositories of what man has believed to be true have either abdicated their authority or lost their credibility. Second, rightly or wrongly, the university, the company of scholars, has so remade man's vision of the world and of himself, has answered so many questions, that in modern man's mind it is now burdened with the task and credited with the ability to provide answers to yet further questions and to remake man's vision of his interior world, of his interior self.

He has no other place to go. He has the university community alone now to fall back upon. Most importantly, he still has his ultimate questions.

It is on this ineluctable questioning proper to and inherent in every man that the university's responsibility to the inmost life of man is founded. As I have briefly suggested, the nature of such a responsibility is not to be confused with that of church or state or family or any other social organ. It is of a nature appropriate to the nature of the university itself, and so must involve intelligence, knowledge, wisdom, in a community of persons.

How such a responsibility ought in general to function I would here like to investigate with you. Obviously, we must begin with the primary concerns of a university—intelligence, knowledge, wisdom. First, and most evidently, the university must take with utmost seriousness its task of the general expansion of knowledge. All knowledge, directly or indirectly, helps ultimately to reach the interior of man. Furthermore, I would say personally as a Christian that such a duty is even more incumbent upon the Christian personally and upon the university which calls itself Christian. Why? Simply from the general logic of the Incarnation, it seems to me. The Christian is committed to this world and to the deepest understanding of it possible, for all the reasons that anyone else can urge, from the alleviation of physical evil to the increase in purely speculative knowledge, simply because knowledge is eminently good in itself. But beyond that, for a Christian, man and the world take on even further significance. This world is not only valuable in itself, but it is transvalued by God becoming incarnate in it in Christ. Not only is man the highest of human goods and a value unto himself, but since God became man in Christ, man is now a value even *beyond* himself. We might ask how seriously the university community has taken the expansion of knowledge, even on the most basic level, and to the painful point of resolutely putting in a subordinate position *all* that does not first and foremost so contribute.

Second, and yet more specifically, it seems to me that the university can fulfill responsibility to the inmost life of man by giving in the future much more attention, much more time, yes, and much more money and prestige to those disciplines which more directly deal with man. Please do not misunderstand: I am not suggesting that the university close down its physics facilities or decide to do no more mathematical research, or stop its involvement in geology or any other such discipline. But I am saying that since our resources are not unlimited and since not all things can be done to an equal degree, it may well be that the university might better turn far more attention than in the past to such fields as deal with man in community and man in singularity. If we took as seriously as we ought the ultimate questions that man asks, should we not find out more about man himself, in psychology, in sociology, in genetics, in cultural anthropology, in economics, in philosophy, in political science, and in history? Perhaps, and it is only a perhaps, the university can best serve man by more concentration of resources herein than it has given to such studies in the past.

To go further, when we have to choose—I wish we did not have to—but when we do have to choose between a new electron microscope and an acquisition for our art gallery, between a campus computer and a campus fountain, do we hesitate long enough to include in our decisions the factors that make for man being more deeply man in the presence of beauty?

But all of this, valuable as it might be, is still essentially peripheral to the intellectual discipline which deals with the inmost life of man as it engages itself in relation to that which is both closest to that inmost life and which at the same time is utterly beyond it, God. I mean, of course, theology, in its widest meanings and in all its varied parts. To recall for a moment what I mean by this "inmost life," we need only recall that we do ask ourselves "What is the universe *doing?* Where did this 'I' come from, this 'I' that no one else can say, this 'I' which is just that personal and equally fragile, and yet upon which for me all the rest depends? What difference does it make what I do, and why do I want others to approve of what I do? Finally, what possible reason or meaning does death, the extinction of this personal 'I', contain?" We ask these questions now. Man has always asked them. Because they get at the inner heart of man, we have no reason to believe he will not continue to ask them, century upon century.

I do not suggest that of itself theology, or even the busy and arduous study of it, will yield the final answers satisfying to this "I" that is myself. Why this is so I shall come to presently. But I do affirm that this subject can and does address itself directly to the questions, that it can and does have something ordered and coherent and intelligent to say about man and his situation, and that pursued in conjunction especially with the other disciplines that treat of man, it can and does illuminate the human condition.

To do so, however, such studies must be undertaken and carried on at the same level of scholarly competence, rigor, devotion and humility as are other university fields. It would seem to follow then that if the university is going to be true to the existential situation of man, it will have to take such studies seriously and sympathetically. On the other hand, if theology is seriously to help meet—not meet, but *help meet*—man's inmost needs in a world society in which knowledge is becoming increasingly complicated, sophisticated, and interrelated, I do not see how it can begin to do so except in the context wherein these attributes of knowledge have been most seriously developed and investigated, that is, within a university context.

Theology must be researched, studied, developed, criticized, transmitted, within the vital milieu of the modern university. We can only rejoice at the recent and planned integrations and re-integrations of theological faculties into total university communities, and at the increasing support given to such studies by universities fortunate enough already to have them. We must also hope that other universities will experience their incompleteness without such studies.

But much more remains to be done. Among the most important tasks are two which have far-ranging implications. First, the university must exert every effort to initiate and encourage inter-disciplinary studies of the sort that will bring ultimate questions into confrontation with more proximate problems and findings. Full many an over-arching theory can fall under the accumulated weight of humble empirical evidence to the contrary. More than one theological proposition may be better off—and the men who hold that it illuminates man's condition better off, too—if it and they enter into relation with other truths which throw a far different light on that same condition. The more they who seek to structure and order possibly ultimate answers enter into commerce with those who look for the structure and order of man and the world here and now, the better off both may be. It does not mean that whole-hearted acceptance of each other's insights will follow. But at least each may become increasingly aware of the complexity of man and the difficulty of communication across the gulfs that separate not only different structures of knowledge but the men themselves who often so genuinely want to communicate. We are often dimly aware of asking the same questions, even if we find so desperately that we are not speaking the same language in asking them.

If this is true of inter-disciplinary studies in which the theological disciplines are to play a serious part, it is perhaps even more necessary that the university put its prestige and its resources behind what might be called inter-ideological studies. By this I mean teaching and research not only in such subjects as the philosophy of religion or the sociology of belief or the history of theology, but also comparative religion studies, and comparative value system studies, not at all excluding but rather welcoming specifically non-theistic systems such as ethical humanism. Surely the religiously committed universities of this country should be beyond the stage where they think they have nothing to gain from the men who seriously attempt to confront the human dilemma on the purely human level. Sometimes the poignant realization by such scholars that this is the only level to which they hold can give added intensity to their search. Likewise, one can hope that the "secular," religiously "non-committed" university recognizes or is coming to the recognition that non-commitment is in itself a philosophical stance open to serious investigation. In addition, the calm and reasoned commitment to a faith or vision of life on the part of many unambiguously qualified members of the academic community argues for an attempt to treat such commitments sympathetically, and to take them seriously in a continuing scholarly investigation of the values we live by, values which are often religious.

Perhaps most importantly, the university community of the Western world will have to open itself much more not only to its own Western religious and ethical heritages, but to those of other cultures and other civilizations too. Other men in other climes have asked themselves the same basic questions we have, and sometimes different ones too, but in answer to them they have come up with sets of symbols and values which structure a life meaningful to them in utterly different ways than those to which we are accustomed. Why? What are those symbolic forms, those configurations of values, so foreign to us, so meaningful and satisfying to them? Why do they provide answers? How do they differ from ours? How are they similar? What can we learn from them in order to penetrate man's inmost life from directions and in ways yet undreamed of by us? The university, if it wants to help man get at himself in depth, will have to do much more in the study of world religions. With some few honorable exceptions of long duration, we have barely begun to provide this help.

In summary so far: we are participants in a world wherein there has been a phenomenal growth in our knowledge of the physical universe, of man and his life world, a world wherein we have both exteriorized and interiorized knowledge, a world wherein we are increasingly involved in an organized thrust into the future and wherein we see the ever-increasing possibilities of creating and recreating the internal and external conditions of our own human lives. With all this we are also

seems to have a special advantage and a special problem. For as Ortega y Gasset once remarked:

> Life consists in giving up the state of availability. Mere availability is the characteristic of growth faced with maturity. The youth, because he is not yet anything determinate and irrevocable, is everything potentially. Herein lies his charm and his insolence. Feeling that he is everything potentially, he supposes that he is everything actually.[1]

It is the advantage of the younger person that his personal vocation is still before him, his self is still open to being fashioned. It is his problem that such an openness leaves him vulnerable. He is vulnerable to a counterfeit structure or to the refusal to structure his life at all. He is most vulnerable to the dehumanizing and demoralizing effects of disillusionment with a community and its members who profess knowledge but ignore wisdom, who discourse learnedly but live meanly, who commune with the great minds of the past and expound the great discoveries of the present but who refuse to respond to the questing *persons* of the present and sneer at, or worse, ignore their hopes for the future.

If for the young this is how the university appears to them, is it any wonder that they react as they do? For so many there is nowhere else to look for ultimate personal answers; they come to the university in search of them and not finding even a personal concern for them or their quest they turn despairingly against a structure which to them seems a fraud.

On the other hand, the teacher in such a community has a special opportunity and responsibility. His it is in the first place to present in his teaching, but even more in his life, the concrete options, the real possibilities, the incarnated actualities which are among the varied images of man, and an encounter with which the student can structure his own self. The response to our potentialities lies only within, at the very deepest interior of ourselves. But the call comes from without. We truly know that we *can* be only in what we actually *are* in our response to each new situation.

If the old institutions, the old, inherited structures of family and church and nation and culture often enough today seemingly cannot provide for society, and especially for the young, the future of society, the situations, much less the answers wherein they find images of authentic man, perhaps the university can, as a shared community of learning and meaning. We all know that a university cannot tell its members *how* to think. We also know that it has a long history of *helping* them to think. I would suggest that the university should do more: it should *help* the student, it should help all its members, to *think and* to *feel* about matters of importance.

It can only do this in a shared contact with the lived concerns of those members. That is all very well in the abstract. In the concrete it means that the university provide structures for such sharing, from more sympathetic faculty to less barracks passing for residence halls, from availability of counselling to specific involvement in our urban ghettos, from a physical environment if not of beauty at least of harmony, to defense of unpopular dissent. In the concrete it means the university taking seriously Plato's remark that the unexamined life is not worth living. It means the university living in its members a critical life, informed, regardful of facts, generous and intelligent, but also willing to analyze, examine, study, and evaluate not only our society at large or even the university at large that becomes too easily what Dickens calls "telescopic philanthropy." Such a shared contact in the living concern of the members means generous and critical examination and evaluation of ourselves too as university persons, as persons simply. How often does the university community help its members to think and to feel about matters of importance? How often does it help a man to grow in the capacity for a truly moral judgment, a response of the whole person to a particular situation? How often is the university even aware that for the young today the great need is for communities of vision and sustenance, and that today perhaps the university is the one community which might provide this?

No university of itself, or in its courses, or in its members can give a perfectly complete or adequate image of man, either in the conceptual and abstract description of the human condition as in philosophy, or in ideal types as in sociology, or even in the more concrete representations of a great work of literature. No one of these will ever represent of or by itself authentic human existence. But then, of course, there is no such thing as a generalized human existence. There is simply *man*, recognized in myself, in other men, and in and through the concrete, unique, single persons who realize their humanity by responding to the call of others in the one, unique, personal way that each of them can do so. Each of us structures his own image of man. Each does it in part alone and in part ineluctably bound up with his life communities. Each of us is involved in a search to understand himself in order that he might become himself. Each of us looks for an authentic and personal humanity which is true both to all that is common to man and unique to me.

All men do this. André Malraux once said that "the greatest mystery is not that we have been flung at random between the profusion of the earth and the galaxy of the stars, but that in this prison we can fashion images of ourselves sufficiently powerful to deny our nothingness."[2]

No man does this by himself, and the same reasons, mentioned earlier, which have today made of the university a unique help to man in his search for truth also obtain for man in his search for meaning. On the other hand, any university committed to man fully as he is will have to play its role in this part of man's task too.

If this is applicable to any university, and I submit that it is, then it is even more applicable to a committed university. Of course, such a university can conceive of the carrying out of its commitment in a propagandistic way, in the arbitrary closing out of options, in the construction of a fully-answered universe, in the fashioning of a ready-to-wear image of man. But then it is not a university and need not at all concern us here. Even a university committed to the Christian faith can so act. But then it too, whatever else it might be, is not a university. So let us pass it by also.

On the other hand, a university committed to the Christian faith can, first, recognize openly, and indeed joyfully, that every man so fashions images and so fashions himself in the demands of the other and in his unique response to such demands. Secondly, it can with equal joy and openness present to him in its own contemporary witness to Christ one who is totally other, God Himself, and who thus makes total demands, and yet one who has in his unique response to those demands of the other fulfilled all of his own potentialities for truth, for meaning and for personhood. In turn, Christ and the Christian witness is not a fixed model or set pattern. Rather, we would say that Christ is our best encounter, the one in which we have the best possibility of fashioning our own unique response of truth, of meaning and of personhood.

In the inmost life of man, as Raymond Nogar has said, "it is not the events of time and space which make all the difference, as though the cosmos were providentially unfolding like a great machine, grinding out human destiny in accordance with unalterable laws. It is the value which you as a free and creative person assign to the things that happen."[3]

Today the university has an opportunity unlike that of any earlier time. As a company of scholars over the past centuries it has shared in the remaking of man's vision of the world. As a community of scholars, mature and apprentice, it can share even more fully in the remaking of man's vision of his *interior* world. It can, if rightly structured, help man not only to think deeply but also to feel deeply about matters of importance. It can help provide the atmosphere in which values can be assigned freely and creatively to our circumstances. Insofar as it helps us bear the twin and personal responsibilities of truth and meaning, the university will become fully *it*self as we become fully *our*selves in our inmost life.

*Delivered at the University of Notre Dame, 1967.*

*This speech was printed in a book titled* The University in a Developing World Society *and appears here with the permission of the University of Notre Dame Press.*

## NOTES

1. José Ortega y Gasset, "In Search of Goethe from Within," *The Dehumanization of Art and Other Essays* (Princeton: Princeton University Press, 1968), p. 169.

2. André Malraux, *Les Noyers de l'Altenburg* (Paris: Editions Gallimard, 1948), pp. 98–99. Quoted and translated in Edward Gannon, *The Honor of Being a Man* (Chicago: Loyola University Press, 1957), p. 131.

3. Raymond J. Nogar, *The Lord of the Absurd* (New York: Herder & Herder, Inc., 1966), pp. 108–9.

# 5

## Toward Renewal:
## The Development of
## Catholic Higher Education

Three years ago, in discussing the responsibility of American
Catholic higher education in meeting national needs, I suggested the need for an objective, carefully prepared, flexible
blueprint for the general development of Catholic higher education in this country. The preparation of such a blueprint
obviously implied the need for objective, carefully prepared
information on the current status of Catholic higher education.

Three relevant research efforts have been initiated since my
remarks three years ago. The recently published report of the
Danforth Commission on Church-sponsored higher education
contains both descriptive and directive information of special
relevance to Catholic institutions.[1] Father Andrew Greeley is
preparing for publication a study of factors relating to the
process of change in Catholic colleges and universities.[2]

Finally, a study of Catholic higher education, sponsored by this Association, is nearing completion. Since I have been closely associated with this last study, I would like to bring you up to date on its progress.

In early fall of this year, a *Working Paper* was distributed to all Catholic colleges and universities, and to all major religious superiors, summarizing the problems within Catholic higher education, as reported by the institutions themselves. This *Working Paper* has been the subject of discussions at each of the regional meetings of the College and University Department and at several regional meetings of major superiors of men.

The final report, to be published in late summer, will incorporate the strengths of Catholic higher education deliberately excluded from the *Working Paper*, and suggest positive steps that should be taken for the future.

As you may recall, the *Working Paper* summarized present impediments under six headings: inadequate financial resources, the dominance of religious orders, organizational insularity, the lack of professional skill, traditionalism, and lack of definition. These were the problem areas most frequently mentioned by the 1500 interviewees on some 100 Catholic campuses.

In addition to the strengths and weaknesses of the Catholic institutions, the research team also found verification of an obvious but frequently forgotten fact: Catholic higher education in this country is a collection of institutions, not a system. In other words, Catholic higher education today is only as strong or as weak as the individual Catholic institutions. The strengths and the weaknesses, the success and the failure, the problems and the potential of Catholic higher education are none other than those of each of the colleges and universities. Obviously, then, when the question is asked, "How strong is Catholic higher education?" the only correct answer is: "As strong as the best Catholic institution and as weak as the worst."

As we look to the future, this contemporary fact of the non-existence of a Catholic system of higher education raises a basic question. Will Catholic higher education continue to be simply a collection of individual institutions or in some way a system or a system of systems? Or, in other words, will the future strength of Catholic higher education depend only on the strength of the individual institutions or will it also derive from systematic coordination?

I hope its strength will come from both. The promise of our future lies both in the growth of individual institutions and in a higher level of achievement through coordinated planning.

First, at the institutional level, I would like to point out examples of steps that are already being taken to insure the strengthening of our colleges and universities through the eradication of institutional weaknesses.

The *Working Paper* pointed out that the most frequently repeated problem for our colleges and universities is the lack of adequate financial resources. Regardless of the size of the institution, its complexity, or the effectiveness of its development office or program, each and every one of our institutions continually faces problems resulting from financial limitations. There is no easy solution. However, recent studies by the Council for Financial Aid to Education seem to furnish some evidence that the weakness I pointed out three years ago, namely, the lack of consistency in building up strong development programs and departments, is gradually being overcome by at least some of our Catholic institutions. As an example of this evidence, if one considers Catholic men's and women's colleges with enrollments between 800 and 2,000 students, some encouraging facts emerge. Among the men's colleges, institutions such as Bellarmine, Gannon, King's, Loras and St. Benedict's have over the past five years generally increased their annual support from corporations, alumni, friends and foundations. Similar solid growth can be detected in such women's colleges as St. Teresa, St. Mary's of Notre Dame, St. Catherine, Mount Mercy and New Rochelle. In most of these colleges the gifts from some of these sources, particularly from friends and foundations, may vary considerably from year to year, as would be expected. But if one looks at the span of the last five years, the conclusion seems clear that the total gift income is consistently reaching a higher level. This is strong evidence that the fund-raising program possesses the essential quality of continuity.

A second problem mentioned by the interviewees was the dominance within institutions of members of the controlling religious order. While there have been compensating advantages to the willingness of the various religious orders to shoulder the responsibility for most of our Catholic colleges and universities, and while the history of achievement in Catholic higher education has been written in large measure by religious men and women, I am convinced that the future depends on increased participation by laymen in both the control and administration of our institutions. The University of Dallas and Sacred Heart University in Connecticut are but two examples showing that Catholic higher education can be directed effectively and efficiently without the dominance of any one religious order.

Further, since our announced change in the structure of the governing board of trustees of Saint Louis University, I have been deluged with letters either calling my attention to the present involvement of laymen on the boards of Catholic colleges and universities or asking for detailed information with regard to possible board changes in other institutions. It is clear that dominance by religious will be replaced by shared responsibility by religious and laity in Catholic higher education.

The lack of definition in Catholic higher education is a problem that has always been with us. Whether a statement of the rationale of Catholic higher education, agreeable to each and every institution, can or even should be attempted is a matter for debate. My concern at the institutional level is the need for precise, realistic, researched, honest, and relevant definition. It is encouraging to note that many of our colleges and universities are seriously working toward such definition, particularly in the use being made of comprehensive ten-year projections. Were the thoroughness, sophistication and comprehensiveness of the self-study at Mundelein College in Chicago imitated by each of our institutions, the lack of definition in the *Working Paper* would quickly be corrected.

Again, although traditionalism still handicaps many of our colleges, there is much evidence that habitual approaches to hitherto unquestioned methods of implementing goals are now being critically reviewed. In the area of Theology, for example, results of a survey by the Association of American Colleges' Commission on Religion in Higher Education revealed that experimentation in this area is more daring in Catholic-related institutions than in other Church-related colleges and universities. Inter-disciplinary courses involved shared faculty are in effect at Marylhurst College in Oregon, Madonna College in Michigan, and Trinity College in Washington, D.C. Ecumenical programs have been initiated, to cite only two examples, at Albertus Magnus College in Connecticut and Loretto Heights College in Colorado.

There are, then, many examples of steps being taken by our Catholic colleges and universities at the institutional level to insure greater enhancement of quality for the future. Through continued individual effort to increase the sources of financial support, to more deeply involve laymen, to develop more meaningful curricular programs through daring experimentation, our future can be a bright one.

However, despite the promise of strength implicit in the effort of individual Catholic institutions, I am convinced that the most critical determinant of the future quality and success of Catholic higher education will be the degree to which institutions involve themselves in coordinated planning.

I have suggested, briefly, ways in which the problems of lack of financial resources and lack of definition are being attacked at the institutional level. I would now like to add the potential for minimizing these same two problems through supra-institutional effort.

It is obvious that our resources will continue to be limited. There is simply not the money available for each and every existing Catholic institution to realize its true potential. Our hope rests in each college or university realistically setting an objective within the reach of its resources. This means that no institution will be able to do everything. Consequently, ways will have to be found to see that neighboring Catholic institutions genuinely complement one another. The unnecessary drain on manpower and money resulting from senseless duplication of programs and facilities must be corrected. Institutional coordination would enable us to accomplish much more than the isolated efforts so typical of the past.

One of the problems cited in the *Working Paper,* which I have not yet mentioned, is that of organizational insularity. This weakness relates directly to problems that must be resolved on a supra-institutional level. The basic isolation of one religious order from another, even the operational autonomy among provinces of one religious order, has resulted in local, regional and national patterns of Catholic institutions having no logical, unifying rationale. The advantages of diversity which can be traced to this insularity are now outweighed by the disadvantages of scattered effort and resource dissipation. While five or six Catholic institutions in one city may reflect the flexibility and variety within Catholic higher education, they also suffer from their isolation. I would like to suggest that were this organizational insularity broken down, through greater coordinated planning, not only would there be more efficient use of resources, but an added advantage of more meaningful definition. Were each institution able to include in its defined objectives the precise role it plays in complementing other institutions, the total Catholic higher educational effort would be more meaningful, and I venture to say, much more successful.

Because of my deep concern over this problem of unplanned and unpatterned effort and because of my conviction that coordinated planning is the key to our future, I would like to suggest a practical plan of action.

Let me first state emphatically that my remarks do not imply that I think this coordination should be imposed on our institutions from without. Rather, it must be done voluntarily, enthusiastically, from the conviction that what most contributes to the development of Catholic higher education is what ultimately determines what is best for each institution. Not vice versa.

My first recommendation is that each Catholic institution—whatever its size, its clientele, its programs, its resources—adopt an attitude of openness to investigating possible alternatives of coordination. This openness should have no predetermined limits. Realizing the full potential of coordinated planning implies a willingness to consider even fundamental structural changes. If an institution sets limits on the type or level of cooperation, little good will be accomplished. The first practical step then, is for all of the Catholic institutions in a given geographic area—particularly the same city or region—to adopt an openness to the possibility of coordinated planning.

Secondly, the institutions within this area should agree, on a voluntary basis, to conduct a feasibility study directed toward a creative answer to the question: "Given our combined financial and manpower resources, our existing and potential facilities, our special talents, what forms of structural organization would be most efficient and effective in accomplishing the area goal of Catholic higher education?"

The answer might suggest any one, or a combination, of several possibilities.

First, relatively minor structural changes. For example, joint faculty appointments, student exchange, or shared facilities. Cooperation of this type is now being effectively utilized by over 40 per cent of our institutions according to a study made in 1964.[3] The proved success of the St. Thomas–St. Catherine–

Hamline–Macalester Program and the promise shown in the plans of Bellarmine and Ursuline in Kentucky are but two of the many examples of this type of cooperative effort.

At a second and deeper level, coordination may suggest mergers with retention of identification. This pattern is being studied by Marymount and Loyola in Los Angeles, and by Immaculate Heart College in Los Angeles in its proposed move to the Claremont College Group. Both of these could be significant moves for Catholic higher education. I could see tremendous good resulting from an experiment involving a Catholic federation of institutions in some one of our larger cities. It is my surmise that were a number of feasibility studies conducted, the federation would emerge as an ideal pattern.

Finally, coordinated planning might suggest the desirability of an actual merger, either with loss of identification by one or more of the institutions, or by all, with the creation of a new institution. This pattern is being seriously considered by Lewis and St. Francis Colleges in Joliet, Illinois, and may be a landmark for Catholic higher education.

I have suggested that our Catholic institutions at the local level adopt an open attitude toward possibilities of coordination and that they jointly undertake, on a voluntary basis, a feasibility study to provide alternatives. I also strongly urge that each institution have the wisdom, courage, and generosity to implement changes that may be necessitated. The year that sees the beginning of genuine internal coordinated planning will be the year Catholic higher education takes a giant step in the direction of excellence.

To investigate and try new solutions, we need specific examples and well-informed advice. If local studies such as I have encouraged are undertaken, other geographic areas will have to capitalize on procedures and results. The men who become proficient in area planning must be made available to others. Where experiments fail, they should not be repeated. Where there is success, it should be made known. When we lose our momentum, we should be prodded. The College and University Department of the National Catholic Educational Association is the logical central agency to provide this stimulation, information, and advice. We must see to it that the College and University Department gets support from us to insure that its role as catalytic agent, information center, and consultant, is effective.

A final note. It is my conviction that, despite our problems, Catholic higher education is engaged in a fascinating renewal. New solutions are being studied and bold steps taken. Through the efforts of individual institutions to continue to correct weaknesses and build up strength, and through the implementation of higher levels of coordinated planning, our future should hold great and exciting promise.

*Delivered at Annual Convention of the National Catholic Education Association, 1967.*

## NOTES

1. Manning M. Pattillo and Donald M. Mackenzie, *Church-Sponsored Higher Education in the United States* (Washington, D.C.: American Council on Education, 1966).

2. Andrew M. Greeley, *The Changing Catholic College* (Chicago: Aldine Publishing Co., 1967).

3. Sister M. Dolores Salerno, *Patterns of Inter-Institutional Cooperation in American Catholic Higher Education* (Washington, D.C.: Catholic University of America Press, 1966).

# 6

# Realities of Power:
# Higher Education

The word "power" occupies two long columns in Webster's *Third New International Dictionary* and the ten different definitions employ words like "force," "sway," "control," "energy," "jurisdiction," "influence," "might," "domination," "strength" and "command." It is interesting that nowhere does the word "responsibility" appear.

Its absence makes the definitions even more relevant for the so-called "power struggle" now going on at many of our institutions of higher education.

I've had the power of the presidency at St. Louis University for almost twenty years, but only recently have I become aware of that fact. I always thought I had only the responsibility of the presidency.

The disruption on a number of university campuses in re-

cent years has been, to a great extent, a confrontation between those who have the power and the responsibility—the
trustees and the administration—and those who, obstensibly
at least, seek to share only in the power. As the president of
the student body of our sister institution in St. Louis—Washington University—declared last year at a conference at the
Center for the Study of Democratic Institutions: "Were
Washington University to be turned over to the students and
faculty, it would fold in about six months because nobody
would know how to run it."

That is, of course, an oversimplification of what is involved
in these campus upheavals, but it is certainly a factor.

Nevertheless, beneath all of the shouting and the rock-
throwing and the sit-ins and the placard waving lie some very
legitimate pressures for change in the patterns of governance
of our educational institutions.

I would like to consider these trends as they relate to the
two principals in many of the recent campus disturbances—
the trustees and the students. Because of the diversity of our
educational institutions, it is difficult to make generalizations
and, naturally, my own reference is St. Louis University, but I
believe that our own experience is relevant to many institutions.

Let's consider first the trustees. Their role varies widely,
depending upon the institution. At some they are considered
largely "window dressing," selected for their name and their
financial resources. At others they have real responsibility for
the destiny of the institution. There is grave danger in giving
trustees only superficial control of the institution. Their interest in the serious problems of the institution is correspond-
ingly superficial, and this may be reflected, for example, in
some of the student uprisings we have seen. The "generation
gap" between trustees and students is definitely more than
one of age alone. I am afraid that in some cases it represents
a failure on the part of the trustees to involve themselves
closely with the problems and aspirations and ideals of the

students who fill the campuses they control. In the home, the generation gap between father and son is often expressed by the statement, "My father doesn't understand me." I believe the student can say the same for many trustees. Some will argue, of course, that the job of interpreting the students to the trustees belongs to university administrative officers, but that is too facile an excuse for relinquishing the duty to make personal contact with at least some students.

Though the student-power movement has produced some obviously undesirable results, in my opinion it has also accelerated several very constructive movements, one of which is reappraisal of the role and obligations of university trustees. I spoke three weeks ago at an Institute for New Presidents sponsored by the American Council on Education at Pennsylvania State University. The discussions with this group and the experienced consultants involved in this Institute deepened my conviction that there is a sharp trend to involve trustees much more directly in policy-formation and to insist that they have a more intimate understanding of the operations of our educational institutions. Nowhere is this more evident, even revolutionary, than in the private, especially church-related institutions.

Traditionally, Catholic colleges and universities have been governed by boards of trustees consisting entirely of members of the religious orders or diocesan authorities that owned the institutions. If laymen had any voice in their operations they were relegated to advisory boards of trustees which provided prestigious rubber stamps for decisions already made.

In addition to the student-power movement, several other factors joined forces to create a climate demanding rapid, sweeping changes. Many Catholic colleges and universities, like my own, are urban institutions, no longer surrounded by seminary-like walls, but deeply involved in the affairs of the community. The Vatican Council, with its exhortations on ecumenism and the role of the layman also has profoundly influenced these institutions. Their constituencies have grown to include business, the professions, community, alumni of all faiths. Should not the policy-making body of the institution truly represent the various interests and needs of these constituencies? As traditionally constituted, the boards of trustees at Catholic colleges and universities consisted of clergy who also served as administrative officers, so, in effect, they were overseeing their own performance and the implementation of their own policies. Obviously, this was not in keeping with modern university practice. Moreover, crucial financial decisions and projections were being made by a group of men who typically had little or no direct experience in business transactions, and who, as a matter of fact, had taken the vow of poverty.

With apologies for the personal reference, let me demonstrate how the influence of these factors just mentioned operated in the case of my own institution. The thirteen Jesuit priests who comprised the board of trustees at St. Louis University voted last year to institute a radical change in the composition of the board of this 150-year old institution. They elected five of the thirteen to remain on the board, including the president and the four vice-presidents, and voted to give equal membership to eighteen laymen, representing various faiths, and to five Jesuits from other institutions. They stipulated that the chairman of the board should be a layman.

This board of 28 has been in operation for a little more than a year, and its involvement and effectiveness has surpassed our most optimistic hopes. Some skeptics greeted our announcement of the board as another example of window-dressing. It has proven to be anything but that. The board members have immersed themselves in the problems of the University and have recommended solutions. The fourteen businessmen on the board deliberate on the future of the University as seriously as they do on that of their own companies. Acutely aware that they have legal responsibility for the operations of the institution, they have made decisions that have helped to strengthen it and keep it on course.

Committees of the board meet regularly, and four times a year the full board meets for two days of intensive sessions.

I should point out that, in reorganizing the board of trustees of St. Louis University, we did not change the character of the university as an institution affiliated with the Catholic Church. The move was definitely not one of secularization, under which the university would become a non-sectarian institution, but a drastic reorganization aimed at better achievement of the academic objectives of the university.

St. Louis University was the first major Catholic university in the country to give laymen a dominant voice on its board of trustees. Since then, a number of other Catholic colleges and universities have adopted similar plans of reorganization, and the trend continues. It may well come to be that these Catholic institutions which, until last year, were insular in their governance and power structure, will set an example for some other institutions that have had heterogenous but largely honorific boards since the day of their founding.

Let us turn now from the question of the role of the trustees in the power structure to that of the role of students. I think it's significant that on that historic day when our new board of trustees gathered for the first time, the evening was spent talking with elected representatives of our 11,500 students. The trustees exchanged ideas and opinions with these student leaders, among them some so-called activists, and I can think of no better orientation for the trustees in preparation for the job that lay before them.

I say that, because I firmly believe that effective governance of colleges and universities today must assimilate the thoughts, the ideas, the motivations and the frustrations of the students, for whom the institution essentially exists. To go one step farther, the institution exists for the benefit of society, and these students reflect that society, for better or worse.

We make a serious mistake if we wave off these campus upheavals as the outbursts of a few misguided radicals. The agitators, of course, represent less than 2 per cent of the total collegiate population, but if there are no roots of discontent among the general student body, how is it that they are always able to win the support of such a large number of their fellow students?

We must face the fact that the college students of today are more intelligent and more committed than the students of, say, five years ago and that the most vocal and vigorous of them are, according to a national survey, generally among those graduating magna or summa cum laude.

In describing these students as "committed," I am referring to their dedication to several causes, particularly social justice and the end of man's inhumanity to man. Of 71 episodes of student disturbances since October 1966, 68 were protests against the war in Viet Nam or racial injustice or both.

Even though we reject their methods of protest, we must not miss the underlying fact: Like a great many older citizens, students in large numbers are convinced that these basic problems in our national life are symptoms of a society that is not healthy. Since they are primarily in contact with colleges and universities as institutional agencies of that society, they strike against the target most available, the university, because they feel it mirrors the ills of the broader society.

If this analysis is true, and I think it is, then those of us of an older generation will inevitably ask: why should students today be so obsessed with their concern for society? Why is their behavior so unlike that of students in earlier generations? Let me suggest three reasons: in the first place there is persuasive evidence that in this country the age of biological maturity now comes earlier than it used to, probably as a consequence of improved diet and medical care. As a result, students begin their college careers with as much as three years more of physiological maturity than was the case for freshmen in 1900. Secondly, those who are graduating today are demonstrably superior in the range of information they command as compared with that of their parents at college age. I'm not saying they are necessarily wiser, but they do know

a great deal more. Thirdly, as never before, they have become a force to conjure with in American society, partially
because of their sheer numbers and partially because of the
sense of group identity and group solidarity that these young
people enjoy in a higher degree than ever before, helped
immensely, of course, by the rapid communication of newspapers, above and underground, and news-weeklies, and especially by TV.

Added to these differences in today's students, the institution's problem is compounded by the fact that it teaches in its
classrooms respect for the dignity of the individual human
person and the lessons of history concerning war. Universities
also share the concern of their students over the short-sighted-
ness and the inequities of the present Selective Service System. How then can we condemn some students for actively
seeking objectives that we all want—peace in Viet Nam,
racial justice at home, and improvements in the draft law? We
can't. We can only condemn some of their methods, many of
which deny the justice and freedom they are intended to
achieve.

But herein lies our dilemma. On the one hand, I don't see
how American institutions of higher education can any longer
tolerate the civil wars that were waged on some of our
campuses last year. I would hope that, before the new semester begins, all will have adopted policies to deal swiftly and
fairly with campus demonstrations that deny the rights of
others in the academic community.

St. Louis University has a policy that says three things:
a) it defines disruptive action as any conduct which restrains
either the freedom of expression or movement of others or
which obstructs normal University operations; b) it states
that any individual or group participating in such disruptive
action will be given a reasonable time to disperse, after which
appropriate officials (campus, or if necessary, city police)
will be called in; and c) students will be prosecuted for
disturbing the peace and will be suspended, and outsiders

will be prosecuted for trespassing. This policy may seem too stern, but the reaction I have received from students is that they welcome it as a protection of their own right to pursue their education. Fortunately, we have never had to invoke the policy.

On the other hand, having protected the students and the institution itself against the illegitimate and destructive activities of students, we still face the task of providing legitimate outlets for their sincere desire to work for a better world. How to achieve this would require another paper, but I would suggest that in general we must work to give our educational programs increased relevance to the problems of life as it is lived today. We must improve the management of campus affairs so as to include students as bona fide members of the academic community, and to provide a higher degree of responsible inter-action between students, the faculty, and the official representatives of colleges and universities.

At St. Louis University we have labored strenuously to merge campus life with the life of the inner city which almost encircles us. As a result our students are expressing their dedication to social justice in many ways. Currently they constitute the single largest source of volunteers for the inner city programs of St. Louis, and they are very active politically, much more so than the students of the so-called "Silent Generation" that preceded them—and this is encouraging for our democratic society.

Within the University we are giving students a greater participation in institutional governance. Last February we added the first students—five in all—to the University Council, a body of 65 members that previously consisted of 42 elected faculty and 23 administrators and deans who serve ex-officio. The council is the highest academic body at the University, and considers matters of general university interest touching on the welfare of the faculty, the welfare of the students and, in particular, the academic operation of the university.

Before appointing the five students, we made a study of similar groups at some 60 universities comparable to St. Louis University in size and complexity. The study revealed, somewhat to our amazement, that only one other university had a voting student member on its council, and that particular university had only one student on its board. I might mention that the five students we appointed were not chosen because they were on the cheer-leader squad for University policies; on the contrary, all are opinion leaders and active in various campus movements.

While we have hardly had time to assess the effects of this move, I believe it is a progressive step and one that might be adopted by more institutions.

In conclusion, I want to express my conviction that the process of decision-making in the power-structure of higher education is undergoing an evolution and, if we have sense enough to see that, we will avoid the revolution that many fear. The administration of our institutions is being democratized, and, if handled with reason and mutual respect, it will benefit us all.

*Delivered before the Advanced Administrative Institute, Harvard University, 1968.*

# 7

## The Imperatives Determining the Future of Jesuit Higher Education

In 1963 when August A. Busch, Jr., announced the goal of $35 million for the next five years and the fact he was assuming chief responsibility as chairman of Saint Louis University's Leadership Council, he said: "It *can* be done; it *must* be done; it *will* be done." This is what I mean by an imperative—something that can be done to insure our future; something which therefore must be done; and moreover something we simply must make up our minds *shall* be done.

I should like to develop the proposition that the future of Jesuit higher education is directly dependent on our ability to carry through on at least seven interrelated imperatives. The vitality and, in some cases, the very existence of our 28 institutions will depend on the degree to which we are successful in achieving these seven imperatives. And it is not so much as a group of institutions that we must act, but as individual colleges and universities.

Three of these imperatives are being faced by non-Jesuit institutions, both public and private, and we share these challenges together. The other four are unique to us as Catholic and Jesuit, and these add to and complicate the sum total of the imperatives we must meet.

In each case, I shall comment briefly on the nature of the imperative itself, the efforts that seem appropriate to meet the imperative; and the present status of our efforts.

## Response to Change and Adaptation

In common with all other institutions of higher education, Jesuit colleges and universities must adopt a style of life that is congenial to change. This requires an internal structure of governance that gives ample opportunity at appropriate levels for *all* of the institutional community to participate in policy formation and execution—trustees, Jesuit and lay administrators, Jesuit as well as lay faculty, students, the entire campus family.

The delegation and diffusion of authority is really in accordance with the spirit of the Society and our earliest traditions. Saint Ignatius urged, and in his own administrative practice demonstrated, that decisions should be made at the level of close contact with reality. "If you lessen the power of the man or group in charge, if you meddle in their business, power is separated from ability with most unfortunate results." In 1553, he sent Father Miguel de Torres as visitor to Portugal. He gave him broad general instructions, of course, but no obligation of proceeding in one way or another. He did give him a large number of blank documents pre-signed so that de Torres could write on them whatever he judged best.[1]

Management consultants who have looked at a good number of our institutions tell me that in many instances we really have not understood nor accepted the principle of the diffusion of authority. We older Jesuits have been brought up in a tradition where religious authority and academic responsibility were identified in the Father Rector, where the principle of obedience to a superior was transferred to our dealings with all inferiors, religious and lay alike.

We have not experienced, nor usually have we been trained in, the organizational system characterized by an orderly process of gathering data, expressing opinion, engaging in debate, weighing pros and cons from all viewpoints, arriving at tentative conclusions, testing their validity, delegating authority to some others whom we hold responsible.

One concrete evidence of a serious institutional commitment to participatory democracy would be the existence and proper functioning of a body, composed of representatives of major segments of the academic community, working on issues of common concern. As of January, 1969, 25 Jesuit institutions indicated that they have such a senate or council with institution-wide functions. Over two-thirds of these have been set up since 1964. The faculty is, of course, represented on all of these senates; the administration is represented on 22 of them, and the students on 15. In most cases, 19 to be exact, the senate does not make final policy decisions but rather recommends policy, usually to the president of the institution.

The response to change in our college and university life must be genuine and sincere. The danger is that we will engage in institutional "tokenism" aimed at satisfying disquieting demands of faculty or students. Our response must spring from the sincere motive of establishing a true community composed of all essential segments of the academic experience.

### Determination and Implementation
### of an Academic Priority System

Whatever objectives or programs we decide to support in our institutions, we will survive only if the financial cost of these is realistically within our reach. This demands a type of planning that has an inbuilt system of academic priorities governing the choices we must make.

Priorities can only be determined by reaching evaluative judgments on the part of those most vitally involved. This means that each institution must have an orderly process for planning the development of its future. A college or university without a clearly defined long-range plan is in trouble, even though it may not suspect it.

Institutional planning is essential. This cannot be stressed enough. It should result in an academic blueprint, which is a photograph of the planning at a particular point in time. Even as the academic plan is being printed, changes render it out of date. The blueprint must therefore constantly be studied and reworked, but it has the value of setting up guidelines and it also gives the institution the ability to control its own destiny. Planning should not be fragmented; it should have an overall plan; there should be a plan for each school or college; and finally there must be a plan for the entire institution. The latter would include general philosophy and purposes, a summary of plans for each academic unit, fiscal projections (not forgetting the annual budget for each year of the projected period), physical needs and the campus plan, and a program for raising the necessary funds.

Just how well are we doing in carrying out the process of academic planning? Information concerning this question was obtained last year as part of a questionnaire related to a master's thesis on the use of cooperative programs in our Jesuit institutions. The researcher, Father James Baker, S.J., asked each of our colleges and universities several background questions aimed at giving a general idea of the status of academic planning in Jesuit institutions. His findings are moderately encouraging. For example, 88 per cent of our institutions said they have made enrollment projections for the next five years; 42 per cent have done the same for the next ten years; 61 per cent have projected their faculty needs and positions for the next five years; 73 per cent have determined their capital and building needs for the next five years; and 70 per cent know their financial requirements and have projected the sources of these funds for the next five years.

However, the weakest area of planning is the most important one of all. I refer to curriculum. In fully half of our institutions, no actual projections regarding new academic programs have been made, even for the next five years.

Unless a Jesuit college or university begins its academic planning with the assumption that its resources in manpower, library materials, and money are unlimited, some system must be devised whereby current as well as proposed new curricular offerings are placed on a priority scale of relative importance on the basis of which the choice or rejection of these programs is determined. I submit that this is the toughest question an institution faces. For what it's worth, here is what Saint Louis University has adopted as its general policy in the matter of priorities.

It is quite clear that, in the light of available resources, Saint Louis University will not be able to attain high excellence in all its programs within the next five years. If all resources were assigned on a mathematically proportioned formula, all programs would be doomed to mediocrity. Hence, the University has adopted a plan of priorities which includes *selective* excellence and different rates of growth and development. The effect of a priority rating will vary with the present condition of the department or program designated. For example, a high priority rating for one department will entail maintaining it at its present level of excellence, with only very limited increase in faculty. In another case, where the department or program is relatively weak, it may demand a considerable expansion and development. Depending upon the plans of the particular school or college, a weak department may be brought up to a level of adequacy, or it may be brought all the way up to high excellence.

Now I would like to move on to a consideration of our institutions as a group, insofar as the effectiveness of our academic planning is concerned. It is my impression, necessarily a superficial one, that most of our four-year *colleges* are increasingly aware of the wisdom of limiting their academic goals and are relatively committed to improving and strengthening their baccalaureate programs without ambitioning to expand into graduate and professional work. In contrast, some of our Jesuit *universities* are already over-extended and are finding it extremely difficult to carry out necessary curricular and program adjustments and curtailment. At the risk of acting the prophet of doom, I would predict that, more than anything else, the decision or lack of it regarding academic priorities will determine the long-range success or failure of Jesuit higher education.

## Exploitation of Every Source of Financial Support

No Jesuit college or university can be satisfied that its future is reasonably promising until it has in operation a program of continuing voluntary support from corporations, foundations, individuals, alumni, parents, faculty and students. Such support will be needed over and above the financial assistance from the federal government which, hopefully, will continue and increase in the years ahead. Jesuit and lay staff must be trained and dedicated to this recognized and respectable area of college and university life.

Twenty years of educational fund-raising have convinced me that there are at least four essential ingredients, one or more of which is too often missing, in the typical support program of our Jesuit institutions:

a) As I pointed out in the second imperative, each institution must have a carefully planned, widely understood and accepted set of academic goals to which are attached realistic financial projections. The fund-raising program has to be a consequence of an accurate blueprint of the institution's academic aspirations.

b) A program for support that operates in fits and starts due to changing institutional leadership is doomed to failure. Thus, a continuum of leadership is essential.

c) Again, many development programs fail because those responsible do not have sufficient faith in their efforts to make the necessary investment prerequisite to successful results. There is no other way; it costs money to raise money.

d) Continuity of leadership, together with willingness to invest, still is not enough without the invaluable advice and aid of lay volunteers. Laymen can advise and act with wisdom and authority only if they are allowed to acquire an intimate knowledge of the college and university for which they are working—one of the most cogent reasons for including laymen on our various boards of trustees. (And the effectiveness of laymen sharing legal responsibility for an institution over those who are merely in an advisory capacity is as different as day and night.)

This would be the appropriate place to urge every Jesuit institution to a more practical realization of the political facts of life. Not only must private colleges and universities seek support from government at the federal level, but also at the state level—particularly in the form of state scholarship programs, tuition equalization programs, and programs whereby private institutions can contract for educational services. A few of our institutions, and particularly Marquette University, have exercised profound influence on state legislation with very gratifying results. Although we have little actual legislation to point to in Missouri, the lobbying and related efforts of the Association of Independent Colleges and Universities of Missouri have pushed us much closer to state aid than we have ever been in the past. We must learn how to use the influence of the institution itself, as well as that of our trustees, alumni and friends, to discover and present an effective case to the key political leadership in the state legislature. Our earlier disdain of political action must be set aside if we are serious about survival.

These are the three essential tasks which we share with all other colleges and universities, especially those under private auspices. We turn now to the four imperatives that are peculiar to us as Catholic and Jesuit institutions.

## The Distinctiveness of Jesuit Higher Education

The fourth imperative is the determination and implementation of the distinctive characteristics of our type of higher education. This, of course, brings us to the key questions in this workshop and the topics which have been most thoroughly discussed up to the present moment.[2] But I would like to emphasize one point previously made, that is, that our distinctiveness as educators in a Jesuit college or university is not to be conceived as a static quality, but like all other elements in the educational process it must be continuously evaluated and reassessed. The 1970 distinctiveness of Jesuit education is not and should not be the same as the distinctiveness of Jesuit education in 1960 or in 1900.

Another point I would emphasize is this: although the 1962 Loyola Workshop also produced some very excellent analyses of the distinctiveness that should characterize our educational efforts, it is more important now than it was then that the present workshop be much more explicit in its determination of means whereby concrete outcomes can be extended into each of our twenty-eight institutions immediately. In this period of educational revolution, it is critically important to provide a structured method for follow-up and evaluation of results, particularly in this area of Jesuit distinctiveness.

I would hope that the Jesuit Educational Association and particularly its Commission on Colleges and Universities will be able to serve as a mechanism for a continuing follow-up of this Workshop so that reports can be made available accurately describing whatever outcomes can be traced to our efforts here in Denver—our efforts, namely, to identify, vivify and activate the current and future commitment of our Jesuit colleges and universities in a world of change. My own feeling is that we have a long way to go in reaching the necessary clarity in regard to the distinctiveness of our educational mission, but, thank God, we are seriously inquiring, even though we are less sure about our results and more humble in our aspirations. I am deeply convinced that our educational distinctiveness can exercise a strong appeal—especially in the light of the backlash being suffered by huge, impersonal institutions, but also because of the general reaction *against* over-permissiveness and the search *for* relevancy and genuine values.

Surely we should be able to present to our students and to the world the kind of institutional climate that would be a convincing answer to Professor Levi's critical evaluation of many American universities:

> There is an obvious correlation between violent student protest and a monstrous size, impersonality in human relations, student neglect, faculty self-centeredness, and administrative remoteness and Olympian grandeur. At Columbia too, the student body is enormous, classes are much too large, the faculty lives in Scarsdale or Queens and hardly knows the university as a place, a locale, a living environment, and Grayson Kirk, its president, spoke only to the Chairman of Consolidated Edison on whose board he sat, the President of IBM whose educational nest he feathered, and the Secretaries of State and of Defense.

> Who can deny today that the university plays a somewhat different role in the family constellation? Somehow in this age of ambiguity and organ transplants, the university has changed its sex. It is no longer the "alma mater"—the nourishing mother—but the "nefarius pater"—the wicked father—and I am afraid largely for reasons which make the rhetoric of "factory" and "corporation" not so irrelevant after all.

> In an article entitled "Universities as Big Business" in *Harper's,* James Ridgeway says: "The universities have been

so successful in safeguarding their privacy—particularly with respect to their finances—that few people are aware of the extent to which the worlds of higher education, big business, and banking are linked through interlocking relationships among professors, college presidents, and trustees, industry and government, relationships whose chief victims are the more than six million students the universities are supposed to teach."[3]

## *Vital Apostolic Relationship to the Society of Jesus*

Our colleges and universities must establish a relationship to the Society of Jesus which will keep our institutions officially and in the eyes of individual Jesuits (especially our younger men), a major apostolate of the Society in the United States. There are certain conditions that would appear to be either essential or highly conducive to the establishment or maintenance of such a relationship.

First, separate incorporation of the Jesuit Community from the educational corporation of the college or university itself. Such separate incorporation provides generous benefits for both sides: it gives the Jesuit Community moral and fiscal identity and viability, and it gives the institution its necessary independence and autonomy. These benefits will not accrue automatically, however, The fact of separation must be preceded by a lengthy, carefully-planned period of orientation and education of the Jesuits involved, so that the process and purposes are clearly understood and so that all Jesuits participate to some degree in the execution of the process. Moreover, in order that the understandings achieved through this orientation period may be preserved for the long future, it is essential that the separate incorporation be bolstered by written tripartite agreements between the Society (represented by the Province), the new Jesuit Community Corporation, and the educational institution.

How is the process of separate incorporation faring across

the Assistancy? My impression is that progress is spotty. There is much hesitancy, largely because of lack of clarity and agreement on the requirements of canon and civil law, and also because of an inadequate supply of expertise in this new field. According to information gathered by the Jesuit Educational Association, as of January 1969, the Jesuit communities had been separately incorporated at only four Jesuit institutions. Fourteen others indicated that such separate incorporation was being planned for completion during 1969. No institution stated that it had definitely decided against the separate incorporation of the Jesuit Community.

I would like to commend to your attention the serious study which has been going on in the Chicago Province, as reflected in the printed report on the Province Planning Program. In the volume entitled "Phase III—Task Force Plans" and dated March 12, 1969, about 70 pages are devoted to the question of "Autonomy and the University," with specific reference to Loyola University in Chicago and Xavier University in Cincinnati.

While I would not agree with every position taken in this statement, it is obvious that a careful effort was made by the members of this task force, consulting with many other Jesuits and laymen, to present all the arguments for and against incorporation and all the conditions which should be guaranteed if the communities at the two universities are separately incorporated. Such careful study and wide involvement can only result in wiser decisions, provided, of course, that the diversity of opinion generated by such discussion does not interfere with a definitive decision in the reasonably near future.

A second element in maintaining a vital apostolic relationship with the Society is the question of present and future availability of Jesuit manpower in our institutions. I believe the situation of the Missouri Province is more or less typical of what we are facing throughout the nation. Assuming that the current number of entering novices remains constant for the next five to ten years, the total number of Missouri Province scholastics will continue its sharp drop of the last five years and will fall from the present 210 to 111 in 1979.

In the case of priests, if an average of 12.6 ordinations per year is projected; an average of 4.4 leaving the Society each year; and an average of 6.6 dying each year, one can project an average annual increase of only 1.6 priests. On this basis, the number of priests would grow slightly over the next decade, from the present 440 to 456 by 1979.

Thus, by 1979, our available working manpower (except for regents) would be about the same as it is today, although Missouri Province Jesuits would be older on the average than at present. Given the likelihood of greater choice of apostolic endeavor, it would appear certain that we will be extremely fortunate if in the decade ahead we can attract the same number, or only somewhat less, Jesuits into our 28 institutions.

But the number of Jesuits in the future is only part of the question. More important is the matter of their attitude towards higher education as an apostolic preference.

Some idea of where we stand on this question appears in survey data gathered for the August 1967 Conference on the Total Development of Jesuit Priests held at the University of Santa Clara. There were 832 college teachers in the sample. This is about 80 per cent of the actual number of Jesuit priests who are college teachers. If these 832 Jesuits were representative of the college teachers in general, we find only 364 (43.7 per cent) who would remain teaching if given a choice; 468 of the priests in college teaching (or 56.2 per cent) *want out into other work*. There were 258 Jesuits in other apostolates who wanted to teach in college but were not, and 132 special students who desire to go into college teaching in the future. These men, added to the 364 who would remain, constitute a work force of 754 men. This is 91 per cent of the size of the present work force.

So you see that there would not be a great loss in *numbers* if college teaching were allowed to individual choice. Yet, if we break it down, we see that only 48 per cent of this new work force would be *experienced,* the rest either coming from other occupations or from among Jesuits currently in preparatory studies. While numbers wouldn't change drastically, the level of experience would certainly drop.

To recapitulate, there were 832 Jesuit college teachers polled in the Santa Clara survey, of whom 364 were satisfied and desired to remain in college work, and 468 who wanted out. There were an additional 258 Jesuits of other occupations who expressed a desire to come into college teaching.

Here are some of the basic findings of the survey: first, if manpower in college teaching were left to attraction, 91 per cent of the present manpower force would be available. Yet, only 48 per cent of this force would be persons now in college teaching.

In contrast, the people who *want into* college teaching are not as well qualified as the people now there. Only 30 per cent have a Ph.D., whereas half of the present force have a doctorate. This group wanting in might have adequate qualifications, however, since 85 per cent have a terminal masters or better. It was also found that this group of people wanting in are late starters and are generally critical of the general course of study and also of their superiors.

The group of college teachers who *want out,* according to the survey, are not as critical of the course but are equally critical of superiors. Half of the people wanting out of college teaching are Ph.D.'s, which indicates that other things besides qualifications are involved in the desire to change occupations. It seems to me that more recent information of this kind is generally encouraging. For example, in its published plan, the New York Province indicates that its Jesuit membership has chosen higher education as one of its principal apostolates.

The information from the Santa Clara survey is, of course,

several years old and in these rapidly changing times may not always represent the attitudes and opinions of Jesuits today.

It seems to me that more recent information of this kind is generally encouraging. For example, in its published plan, the New York Province indicates that its Jesuit membership has chosen higher education as one of its principal apostolates.

In the voting at the Chicago Province Congress (March 29–April 5, 1969) the following propositions were approved by a very substantial majority:

> The apostolate of higher education, whether in presently existing forms or in any of the new forms proposed, should be recognized as one of the most important activities of Jesuits of the Chicago Province. (Y-48; N-10; A-3)

> The Jesuit Community at both Xavier and Loyola University, as well as the various academic and non-academic departments, should take the initiative in encouraging Jesuits to work at these institutions in academic and pastoral capacities. (Y-60; N-1; A-0)

> In planning a university career the individual should give priority to Jesuit universities—especially Loyola and Xavier. (Y-44; N-3; A-14)

To cite another example, the New England Province recently published its "Plan for the Future" in which it is strongly affirmed that the "ministry of higher education remains among the prime areas of Jesuit services." The future of this apostolate in the New England Province is to depend on the implementation of two principles:

> The principle of attraction, i.e., "that the primary responsibility for attracting Jesuit presence rests with the institution or ministry and the Jesuits who service it"; and

> The principle of consolidation, i.e., "that the Province's review of higher education be done with a view to con-

solidating our major Jesuit presence into one, or at most two, of our present three institutions of higher learning.

## Relationship to the Church

Another essential imperative is the establishment of a mutually understood and viable relationship with the structured Church—Rome, the local diocese and its Bishop. Such a relationship must, on the one hand, continue to merit understanding and support on the part of the Church of our institutions as "Catholic" in a bona fide sense, yet on the other hand, be truly independent of the hierarchy so that the college or university can pursue truth in every area of human knowledge, including theology, without hindrance, undue questioning, etc.

It seems to me that very encouraging progress has been achieved in the effort to promote increasing awareness on all levels of Catholicism of the nature of a Catholic college or university. This effort was initiated by the Land O' Lakes statement of two years ago, produced by representatives of American and Canadian Catholic universities; followed up by the statement on the role of the Catholic university in the modern world adopted in Kinshasa, Congo, last September; and then confirmed, at least implicitly, by a lengthy document recently circulated to all Catholic universities as the result of a World Congress of Catholic Universities sponsored by the Congregation on Catholic Education at the end of April of this year in Rome. The position paper representing the consensus of the Congress represents a significant advance in the understanding of what a Catholic university is, both in its commitment and, at the same time, in the autonomy which must necessarily be part of any university.

Let me quote from two of the most important points analyzed in the report. First, regarding the essential characteristics of a Catholic university:

> Since the objective of the Catholic University, precisely as Catholic, is to assure in an institutional manner a Chris-

tian presence in the university world confronting the great problems of contemporary society, the following are its essential characteristics:

1. A Christian inspiration not only of individuals but of the community as well.

2. A continuing reflection in the light of Christian faith upon the growing treasure of human knowledge.

3. Fidelity to the Christian message as it comes to us through the Church.

4. An institutional commitment to the service of Christian thought and education.

All universities that realize these conditions are Catholic universities, whether canonically erected or not. The purpose of the Catholic university can be pursued by different means and modalities according to diverse situations of time and place, and taking seriously into account the different natures of the disciplines taught in the university.

The second point from which I should like to quote concerns the autonomy of the Catholic university and its relationship to ecclesiastical authority:

> The Catholic university today must be a university in the full modern sense of the word, with a strong commitment to and concern for academic excellence. To perform its teaching and research functions effectively the Catholic university must have a true autonomy and academic freedom. Nor is this to imply that the university is beyond the law: the university has its own laws which flow from its proper nature and finality.

Although the evidence of progress is encouraging on some of these fronts, I hasten to warn that we may still find ourselves in a precarious position in the turbulent days ahead. The backlash from statements and actions of liberal theologians is inevitably pushing bishops into a more conservative mood. They want to "get rid" of trouble-makers, and have a period of peace. Cases are multiplying where procedures will be required. Each institution should have its own procedures carefully formulated and backed up with strong theological thinking. Efforts should be made individually, especially by those who understand the problem from the university viewpoint, and by Jesuit institutions corporately, to place these procedures before the bishop, so that the first instance of their application will not come as a shock to him.

## New Relationship with the Immediate Community and General Public

It is imperative that we either vigorously maintain our individual institutions as public-service, community-related colleges and universities, or convert them into such as rapidly as possible. Only thus can we call on the resources of the entire community: lay as well as religious, Protestant and Jewish as well as Catholic, persons from various socio-economic levels, etc. The best guarantee of total commitment to community responsibility is a Board of Trustees representing the community and sufficiently detached from the internal management to be the institution's public "conscience."

In regard to this imperative, it would seem that substantial progress can be reported. With the assistance of local legal authorities and with counselling across the country our institutions have been engaged in widespread changes in their governing bodies. As of January 1969, eleven Jesuit institutions had already received official approval for the inclusion of laymen on their boards of trustees and have actually done so; one had an application pending for such authorization; eight did not intend to establish a mixed board. Of the eight which intend to retain an all-Jesuit board, four include Jesuit board members from outside the particular college or university.

Another aspect of community relationship is reflected in the willingness to do our share to solve the urban crisis in which all of our institutions are more or less involved.

This past May, under the auspices of the Office of Scientific and Technical Information, Cambridge, Massachusetts, the U.S. Office of Education, and the Sloan Foundation, representatives of the administration, faculty and student body of eleven urban universities were brought together with volunteer workers and civil officials from these major cities. The discussions that took place in this three-day conference at Martha's Vineyard produced some ideas which I think we should all ponder in terms of our special urban obligations as Catholic and Jesuit institutions.

First of all, we must examine our urban obligations and involvement as a corporate entity; e.g., the use of our investment portfolio; the local impact of our purchasing budget; our employment policy and practice; our participation in the educational process at the elementary and secondary school levels; our availability as an information resource; our posture as an advocate for the local neighborhood; our efforts at reshaping service systems for the benefit of the inner-city (education, law, business and medicine); the availability of our physical facilities.

Secondly, as an educational institution presumably committed to the solution of our country's most serious social problems, we must see to it that the total academic community—trustees, administrators, faculty and students—are concerned about our goals and the alleviation of constraints upon the achievement of these goals. Key questions in this self-examination would include:

a) Are we increasing access of disadvantaged students to our institutions, or are we letting outmoded credential systems stand in the way?

b) Are we open to experimentation and new forms of teaching, or are we allowing entrenched antiquated faculty control to hinder fresh approaches?

c) Are we adding to our faculty the unique kind of teacher, who can relate effectively to the kind of student who is coming out of the ghetto, or are we allowing an entrenched departmentalism and the privileged position of departmental and

## Summary and Conclusion

faculty power structures to perpetuate the current system?
Here, then, are the seven imperatives which in my opinion are
inextricably bound to the future of Jesuit higher education.
We have a future *if* we are determined to:

1. be open to institutional change and adaptation;
2. establish and carry out an academic priority system;
3. exploit every source of financial support;
4. develop and strengthen the distinctive characteristics
   of Jesuit education;
5. establish a vital apostolic relationship with the Society
   of Jesus and individual Jesuits;
6. Maintain a viable relationship with the organized
   Church; and
7. cultivate a relationship of service and involvement
   with the immediate community and the general
   public.

Admittedly, this is a frightening, formidable agenda. In
honesty, I must admit that my answer to the question, "What
is the future of Jesuit Higher Education?" depends on whether
you consider all 28 colleges and universities collectively or
individually. Collectively, like all private higher education,
the Jesuit system has a rather dim unpromising future in the
light of the thriving, all-inclusive, highly competitive growth
of public institutions everywhere. Individually, however, I
am convinced that many of our 28 institutions have a bright
exciting future, because I am confident that in many of them
there will arise Jesuit and lay leaders—trustees, administrators, faculty and students—who will accept the challenge
of these seven imperatives with vigor and determination
and will fight their way through to ultimate success.

*Delivered before the Workshop* Jesuit Universities and Colleges:
Their Commitment in a World of Change, *Denver, Colorado,
August 8, 1969.*

## NOTES

1. Paul Doncoeur, S.J., *The Heart of Ignatius* (Baltimore: Helicon Press, Inc., 1959), p. 105.

2. Other papers given at the JEA Denver Workshop on "Jesuit Universities and Colleges: Their Commitment In a World of Change," August 6–14, 1969, are to be found published in Eugene E. Grollmes, S.J., ed., *Catholic Colleges and the Secular Mystique* (St. Louis: B. Herder Book Co., 1970).

3. Albert W. Levi, "Violence and the Universities," *Washington University Magazine*, vol. 39, no. 1 (Fall 1968), p. 14.

# 8

# The Wedding of Town and Gown

For the past fifty years, Texas Christian University and the city of Fort Worth have been living and growing and progressing together. At this half-century mark, I think all of us who have gathered here to celebrate this auspicious occasion would be wise to ask ourselves this question: What should the relationship be between an urban university and the community in which it resides? Specifically, what should the relationship be between Texas Christian and the civic, industrial, commercial community of Fort Worth?

Let me first say something about the nature of the urban community in America. Since the end of World War II, we have seen in the United States the climax of a gradual change in our country from a rural to an urban society. Almost two-thirds of our population lives in metropolitan areas, as opposed to one-third in 1900. Accompanying the tremendous shifts in our population from rural to urban areas has been an even more dramatic change in the urban communities themselves.

Today, the urban community consists of a "central city" containing the downtown area, industry, and the older residential districts. This central city is surrounded by suburban communities in which the city workers live and raise their families, partially fulfilling the American dream of country life without giving up the advantages of an urban location. This arrangement so well suits the desires of many Americans that, as shown by the 1960 census, the typical "central city" has declined in population while the metropolitan area itself has gained enormously. However well-tailored this pattern is to the tastes of individual Americans, it has been inimical to their collective interests. Side by side with the pleasant results, fantastically complicated problems have arisen in municipal government, taxation, streets and highways, transportation facilities, juvenile delinquency, elementary and secondary education, and many other areas. The overall problem is so well recognized that both of our great political parties have pledged in their Presidential platforms to take steps to help solve it.

For several years, however, the first citizens in these communities to recognize and tackle this job have been our urban universities. Political scientists, economists, engineers, sociologists, and faculty members of virtually all academic departments have participated with local authorities in working out solutions. In some cases, universities have been able to participate directly in slum clearance and rehabilitation. Saint Louis University, for example, is participating as a private developer by building a twenty-two-acre addition to its campus in the Mill Creek Redevelopment Project in St. Louis, and my Alma Mater, the University of Chicago, has played a leading role in that city's programs for urban renewal and slum clearance. There are many similar examples which illustrate that the urban university in America is not only a good neighbor, but an essential partner in civic progress on all levels.

Only in America is this possible. In Europe and other foreign lands universities have little direct contact with the communities in which they are located. If we trace the histories of medieval universities, or if we study the relationship even today between most of the European institutions and their local communities, we must conclude that the situation can best be described as a cold war, a state of mutual distrust between the town and the gown. No matter what the justification for this historical fact may be in many parts of the world, this definitely cannot be the correct relationship between an American university today and its urban environment.

The role of the urban university in helping its community solve problems of urban growth is, of course, an *example* of the relationship between the institution and the city, not a definition of what the complete relationship should be. Even in a relationship such as we have here in Fort Worth today, I think that some create a false notion of what the city should be to the university and the university to the city.

I have often heard it said—in fact, I have said it myself—that an urban university has two fundamental functions: to teach and to carry on research; and then as a sort of extra obligation, the university also assumes the task of serving its community by adult education programs, institutes and conferences for professional and business groups, consultation in engineering, economics, etc. Although I agree that all these so-called 'services' belong in proper proportion to the central objectives of a university, I should like to argue that these services should be growing out of a much sounder, more integrated understanding of how the university and the community are interrelated.

First let me point out two factors of this relationship which might be called geographical advantages of the presence of an urban university in a city. First, the university provides educational opportunity for those who cannot afford to live away from home while they attend college, and second, the student who attends college in his home city tends to stay there after graduation with the result that the city does not lose many talented and productive citizens who might otherwise settle down elsewhere.

To get a truer understanding of the less obvious factors of this question, let us ask ourselves: what should the relationship be between a university and its individual students? In essence, the university's task is to create an environment in which each individual student may be inspired to develop the best that is in him. Latent within his physical, emotional, mental and moral makeup are potentialities towards the full flowering of which the university surrounds each student with a faculty, a library, and the physical equipment needed to motivate him to that initiative and interest in his own development which alone constitutes true education.

How does the university create an environment ideally suited for the teaching-learning process? On the part of the institution and specifically the faculty, two basic conditions are required: a) instructional programs directly for the benefit of the students, and b) research programs aimed at keeping both the faculty and the student body alive to the never-ending responsibility to pursue truth in every field of human knowledge. But right here at the very core of a university's key objectives is where we may fail to recognize its role in relationship to the outside community. Too often we think of teaching and research as a process affecting only the individual: Professor X teaches this boy or girl a course in history; Professor Y is carrying on research in physics which will improve his own grasp of the field and possibly train this or that graduate fellow in some new technique. This is much too narrow a viewpoint. Although teaching and research are and should be highly individualized processes, in a typical American university today these processes have direct results that reach far beyond the individuals involved. I have been struggling for some phrase that would describe this broader, and I think truer, concept of a university's role. I hesitate to use the term: corporate teaching and corporate research, since it may be too easily identified with the derogatory ideas we all associate with the notion of 'mass education,' the neglect of the individual student with all the differences we know each possesses. I am not advocating the notion of 'mass education'; I am trying to show that the teaching of the individual and the research activities of each faculty member intrinsically involves something more. They are inseparable from the effect they have on the community where they take place. Just as in any other area of human living, what happens to the individual cannot be isolated, nor separated from the community in which he lives.

One of the educational advantages of the urban university is that this realization is much easier for the student and his teacher to grasp, surrounded as they are by life on a vast scale. The community serves as a stimulus to the educational process itself, and at the same time benefits by providing the environment for its accomplishment.

Possibly this intimate university-community relationship can best be understood by developing one or two examples of what actually takes place. Each year in the College of Arts and Sciences here hundreds of individual boys and girls are taught in English classes to express themselves more fluently, more cogently, more clearly. This facility affects not merely their own lives; the entire community with which they come in contact is elevated and improved by reason of their presence. Again, the influence on the city is even more obvious when you realize that each year hundreds of men and women trained in the skills of the teacher, the accountant, the nurse, and many other professions establish themselves in this community as graduates of Texas Christian. The direct immediate result is the uplifting of every aspect of the community— better city government, better health for all citizens, greater interest in cultural values. These college graduates are the leaven which affects the whole mass. Again, a professor here works on some abstruse scientific research problem; eventually he contributes some new fact, let us say, in the field of biology. True, the man in the streets of Fort Worth is not immediately affected, but someday he or his children will possibly be saved by some new medicine which has been developed out of the new fact discovered years before in a Texas Christian laboratory. And so on—the examples could be multiplied.

The point I have been trying to make has been admirably expressed by John Gardner, President of the Carnegie Foundation:

> The role of the universities is undergoing a remarkable change. They are being thrust into a position of great responsibility in our society—a position more central, more prominent, more crucial to the life of the society than academic people ever dreamed possible. . . .
>
> The interesting question is not whether the university will be active in the world of affairs—it will!—but whether, in meeting the demands upon it, it will exhibit qualities of statesmanship or function as a sort of badly organized supermarket. . . .
>
> Any coherent conception of the university's role must begin with an understanding of the university's central missions—teaching and intellectual inquiry. These are the secrets of the university's strength, and the springs of its vitality. To the extent that it allows itself to be diverted from these functions, it is contributing to its own eventual decay as a significant institution. The extramural activities of the university need not impair the university's capacity to carry out its central mission. They may even increase it.[1]

The urban university, therefore, is committed to teaching and research but through these very functions the university betters both the individual and the community simultaneously. In order to protect and promote this essential mission, what

are the respective duties of the university and the community?
On its part, the university has two never-ending obligations:
a) to pursue teaching and research at a level of high excellence; and b) to do so in an atmosphere of dedication to the
basic values of our national heritage.

As to the first obligation, I shall merely charge the administration and faculty and student body of this institution with
a solemn duty of which I trust they are fully aware: the
stability, the security, yes, even the very existence of our
American civilization depends in large measure on the intensity with which you pursue the highest excellence in your
teaching and research.

I am convinced that the second obligation of an urban university needs vigorous re-emphasis today. When we say that
your teaching and research should be carried on in an atmosphere of dedication to the basic values of our national heritage, what do we understand as our American system of
values? The American value system is based on the truths
which were expressed in Galilee two thousand years ago,
restated and embraced almost two hundred years ago by the
Founding Fathers of this republic: the existence of a common Father who created us, the origin from Him of our
human rights and the consequent worth and dignity of our
fellowman, the existence of a moral law which sets forth an
absolute norm on what is right and wrong in human conduct.
Our Founding Fathers were committed to the fact of God
and to their responsibility to His eternal, divine law according to which men and society must live. And today if the
university is to play its essential role in promoting our national purposes, it must thrust all its resources into a supreme
effort to produce graduates who have a personal commitment
to these values.

It is in this atmosphere of total dedication that Texas
Christian and every university must carry on its pursuit of
truth. And as this process of teaching and research goes forward, what is the obligation of the community, the obligation

of Fort Worth, to this university? Again, I shall mention only two aspects of this obligation. First, a community must respect the responsible objectivity and freedom of a university; a university's pursuit of truth must be free and uninhibited. Her duty is to be in the forefront of man's effort to strive for the truth in every human problem and, once the truth is known, to defend it in spite of the unpopularity that may result. Hence, neither the community nor any segment within it, no matter how influential, should ever pressure the university into identifying itself with ideas or policies or practices which are partisan, selfish, stagnant, unfair, or unsound. Business organizations, labor unions, political parties, pressure groups of any kind have no right to expect a university to promote ideas in which they have vested interests. They should be happy, in fact they should insist, that their university have only one dedication—a relentless dedication to the pursuit of truth everywhere and at all times regardless of what the consequences may be to any partisan involvement.

Secondly, there is a positive, more constructive obligation which this community must accept towards Texas Christian University. The maintenance of excellence in the pursuit of truth is an extremely expensive process today, and no university, neither the tax-supported nor the private institution, can achieve its objectives if the cost of the process must be borne by the individual students alone. Today the community must support particularly private education, not from a motive of charity as you support your hospitals, orphanages and other humanitarian organizations (worthy as they are), but because the university's functions of teaching and research are essential to the life and welfare of each and every citizen of Fort Worth. In a true sense this community owes support to Texas Christian as a payment for value received. I tried to demonstrate earlier that the university has the same obligation towards the community generally which it has towards the individual student. And if this is true, then the community as well as the individual student has the correlative obligation of supporting the university. And this obligation is of life-time duration, for the student and future alumnus as well as for all citizens of the community.

It is my experience that the very large corporations, particularly those national in scope, have come to a rather far-seeing understanding of their obligations towards higher education and particularly towards colleges and universities operated under private auspices. But this same sense of responsibility has not penetrated to many other important segments of society—medium-sized and smaller business firms, labor organizations, professional groups who have funds at their disposal, many individual citizens of means who argue that they have no obligations because they have not attended the institution themselves or otherwise had any formal contact with it. No, today with the demands every community places on its universities, with the dependence of every citizen on the work which only universities can carry on, there is no one who can rightfully shrug off a personal duty to do what he can to keep that university strong, vigorous and free.

And so, as all of us pause today to contemplate the blessings of fifty golden years of a life which has entwined Texas Christian and Fort Worth, we of the academic world particularly should carry away with us a new realization of the relationship of the city to the university whose primary objective is to teach and carry on research not merely for the individual student but for the entire community, and to discharge this noble purpose in an atmosphere of total commitment to the enduring values of our Judaeo-Christian tradition. In turn, those who are identified with the civic, industrial, and commercial segments of this community should carry away a deeper realization of their obligation to respect this university's right to freedom in its pursuit of truth, and their obligation to keep Texas Christian strong and vigorous through continuing generous support from every segment of the Fort Worth community.

*Given at Texas Christian University, Fort Worth, Texas, on October 6, 1960.*


## NOTE

1. John W. Gardner, "The University in Our Civilization," *The Education Record*, January 1960. Copyright by the American Council on Education.

# 9

# The Role of Higher Education in Restoring Urban Centers — What We Have Learned

Most of us can recall when America's cities were her joys. It was the turn of the century. Legislative decree had created the world's largest city with the union of the five boroughs of New York. Skyscrapers were piercing the clouds as America's cities reached for the skies. Songs rang out of St. Louis, and on the sidewalks of New York.

True, huddled immigrant masses occupied areas not unlike our present slums. But they were being assimilated. Each year, more and more moved out, moved on into the mainstream of American society.

With the passing of the frontier, America's cities began to reflect her hopes and her ambitions, and the reflection was one of optimism, of seemingly unlimited opportunity for everyone. Even the poorest could rise; it was not a myth—it was the miracle of America.

Today, however, as we know too well, a multiplicity of factors have made of our cities our sorrows. Poverty, racial ghettos, crime and vice, human injustice, and hopelessness predominate where once there was laughter and promise. Traffic problems, smoke problems, health hazards, cry out for attention. The underprivileged—trapped among slums by an absence of opportunity—sit, smouldering in the hearts of our cities. On every side we hear different proposals for what should be done. Charges of vested interests and disagreement fill the air. There is in many areas an inability to act together.

And in all likelihood, things will get worse before they get better.

If they are ever to improve—if our cities are to be revitalized, restored, if all our people are to find again the opportunity and hope that have always been America, it is clear that some force for advancement must be harnessed which cuts across lines of politics, special interest and race. More and more it is becoming evident that this one force, this power to unite and move forward for the common good, is the urban university—that institution which enjoys the necessary intellectual resources in all the disciplines attendant on our urban crisis and which holds (or should hold) the confidence of all those concerned.

Our topic here today then is "Case Studies of the Role of Higher Education in Restoring Urban Centers—What We Have Learned." Our charge is to look at what has been done —to determine what should be done better in the future.

As we know, we have just begun to take this problem in our grasp and, not surprisingly, that which has been accomplished, that which has received widespread attention has also received a fair share of criticism for just that reason. Perhaps we in the universities have been guilty of over-emphasizing the more glamorous aspects of physical redevelopment, instead of concentrating our emphasis on what should be a much larger program.

## Some Beginning Steps

But, setting that aside for the moment, all of us would agree that the urban university's role in restoration must begin with its own commitment to stay where it is in the heart of the city, to provide for itself room to meet the requirements of tomorrow for expanded services, and to insure the proper environment for its work. By and large, we have learned that with planning, cooperation and ingenuity this can be done—to the benefit of the entire community.

We do not have to look far for the examples. Here in Chicago, the University of Chicago has had to perform major surgery on Hyde Park to revitalize its area. Its renewal program is the third largest project in the nation, covering 900 acres and costing approximately $195 million in federal, local and private agency money.

Pockets of deterioration have been cleared out—shopping centers, apartments and town houses have sprung up. Acres have been or will be added to the University of Chicago campus for expansion and for married student housing. In other areas buildings have been renovated, new schools, parks, playgrounds and streets, built—all on non-discriminatory patterns.

In Cleveland, Western Reserve and Case Institute have joined forces with some 34 other institutions to carry out a twenty-year plan to develop a $140 million University Circle. The cooperating institutions have set up a University Circle Development Foundation which can accept tax-free gifts. The Foundation buys property from private owners and then resells it to the member institutions for the prescribed uses. The Foundation also has induced the City of Cleveland to undertake a large urban renewal plan nearby.

Philadelphia's universities are working closely with city-wide development. Each institution is the anchor of a special sub-development of the over-all program. The University of Pennsylvania and Temple are in the forefront.

At Harvard, Wayne State, MIT, and in Los Angeles the story is the same.

From Pittsburgh, a totally new concept for financially-pressed private institutions has emerged. Several institutions in the Oakland area have seized upon a profit-making plan to keep that division of the city a cultural island. The group will build homes, apartment buildings, offices, shopping centers, parking garages, personal service business facilities. A research park—so dramatic in design that it has been called the first building of the 21st Century—has been planned. This research facility will, in turn, provide impetus and attraction for new industry to settle in the area.

Yet, despite these grand designs for physical resurgence, universities have met with widespread misunderstanding. We have learned—to our benefit, I feel—that often plans for superhighways are greeted with more general enthusiasm than our own.

A recent national magazine article points up some of the problems in understanding. The editors point out that since 1947, Columbia and thirteen other institutions have been joined together as Morningside Heights, Inc., and have been working on the problems of crime and squalor in upper Manhattan. The University has encouraged vast housing projects, is spending millions of dollars to buy up and rehabilitate slum buildings, conducts recreation programs for local youth, helps maintain private street patrols, and is inducing new institutions to build in the area.

Yet, despite the war on blight that its activities represent, the magazine continues, Columbia is called by many a greedy neighbor, "bent on swallowing the whole area for itself." Many residents who like the campus atmosphere do not want to be relocated. They resist and protest what they call meager financial and relocation aid. Charges that the school is bent on driving out Negroes and Puerto Ricans, the newcomers, are heard from individuals and civic groups—this because some of the rundown buildings bought and cleaned out by the University were tenanted almost exclusively by Negroes and Puerto Ricans.

Columbia officials, however, consider that the campus and Morningside Heights constitute one of the nation's most thoroughly and successfully integrated areas, with residents of fifty national origins.

Other critics (cited by Joan Colebrook in *The New Republic,* June 15–22, 1963) have charged that urban renewal everywhere has been discriminatory in that wholesale evictions of Negroes and Puerto Ricans have been sanctioned to make way for luxury developments. In most cities, it is asserted, the dispossessed low-income and minority families have had no recourse but to move into nearby marginal areas, thus creating new pockets of deprivation—that with all the bulldozing and building, there seems relatively little concern for the community—for the individual.

These critics point out that since education and re-education are among the great slum needs, the universities ought to provide real civic leadership and spread a cultural web over blighted areas.

With this, I think most of the universities would concur. For the building of a walled city for a university campus can and must be only the beginning—otherwise we have performed no greater service than the private realtor who has added another high-rise luxury apartment unit to the city's skyline. Those who need help most may wonder—and with full right—what has this to do with me?

And if the university has not to do with the meanest, the most insignificant "me" of the slums, it has no right to the title University. For, as most of us would agree, today's urban university cannot live in isolation—for to do so would be to court folly.

It is difficult to believe that any university planners have as their basic objective to *hold the line* against squalor encroaching on their campuses. They may hire police forces to patrol adjacent neighborhoods—but this is only a "stop-gap" measure. They may clear and remodel tenements or demolish them, but this again is only the first step. We in St. Louis may say that the Mill Creek Valley is no longer a rat-infested slum, but this is not enough. Rather, we should ask ourselves— "Where are the other blighted areas?"—"How can we rehabilitate them?"—"How can we rehabilitate their people?"—"How can we see to it that no new slums ever develop again?" We must be ready to remodel, renew and revitalize our urban society.

Perhaps, this is the greatest lesson we have learned. We cannot plant a few trees and hide our problems behind a wall of modern buildings, pretending that they have gone away. This is what I mean when I say that we benefit from the fact that sometimes super-highway projects are more popular than our own rebuilding. It makes us stop and think. Are our efforts as comprehensive and as meaningful as they ought to be? And if they are, are we going about interpreting them in the right way? Perhaps we are not communicating properly with our own internal families, with our public relations officers, with the very people whom we should be striving to help.

Moreover, I think we have learned that this must be a long-range continuing fight. This personal and physical blight is the sum total of the havoc wreaked by all the diseases which prey upon our cities. And just as our schools of medicine continue to fight the ravages of mind and body, so must we be prepared to make war on urban problems as far into the future as our minds can stretch.

Everett Case, President of the Alfred P. Sloan Foundation, put it very succinctly to the Association of Urban Universities meeting in New Orleans last fall: "Urban renewal begins but does not end with slum clearance and well-planned modern facilities; to be significant, it must also involve a kind of re-

programming which go beyond one
-end conferences without depth and v
consequently, without impact upon ur
iversity, he says, must consider the cit
of establishing an academic department
it resides—"for this is the force we m
er with wisdom, we must have knowledg
rban universities must become the intelle
"experiment stations" of this urban age, ar
l better ways of meeting urban life and i
as the land-grant movement provided thes
gricultural America of another time. Despit
ons to science and technology and to nationa
e the larger and larger role they are coming
rican higher education, our urban universities
truly come of age until they accept full re-
leadership in a renewed and revitalized urban

that, unappealing as some of us may find it,
ban life is outside the purview of the modern
sity. Our cities are our last frontiers; what hap-
in the next five, ten, twenty years will in great
ermine what happens to our nation and, yes, to
ee world in our fight for survival, for leadership.
mit our cities to deteriorate, to decay . . .
mit pockets of poverty and discontent to swell and

ontinue to ignore basic human rights and dig-
nothing about the factors which breed vice and
y . . .
rn away from the problem of the unskilled and the
ed . . .
feel that a few dollars for bread, beans and steel
e all we need to contribute . . . then we might as
ender today. For our society, our way of life, cannot

---

newal of the spirit." John Osman of the Brookings Institution has concurred that the ultimate urban problem is an intellectual one, and thus it has to be a *continuing* concern of the university.

What directions might we consider, then, for continuing future action after we have put our own houses in order, after we have planned new campuses and research parks and have done all the things we must for our own internal, physical planning, after we have accepted the notion that we must do more?

We might profitably consider new approaches and greater emphasis on old approaches:

1. We ought to become more active in planning for urban re-development in areas not directly affecting the university as well as those in which our interests are intensive. We should lend all of our know-how—architectural, sociological, behavioral, etc.—to city and private planners as an aid to working out the best possible programs of rehabilitation, demolition and rebuilding—to insure that the rights of all are protected, to make certain that provision is made for the low-income, underprivileged groups that are often removed for middle- and upper-income developments, to make sure that renewal plans include planned communities which afford opportunity for a new life. We might also encourage students who qualify to move into and become a part of these new low-income communities, to make certain that "renewal" will be a reality physically and intellectually. We should lead and "mould" public opinion in support of good programs.

2. Conversely, we ought to oppose and refuse to cooperate in any renewal plans which do not make provision for the rights and interests of all and that do not take into account all of the factors which the university knows must come into play.

3. We ought to pay more than "lip-service" to developing ever-increasing numbers of young people who will bring their talents to bear each in his own specialized way on the core problems of the urban community. We must somehow

wrest the ideal of helping the underprivileged from the realm of platitudes and make of it a way of living for our graduates.

4. We ought to consider sending people out into underprivileged areas. In Saint Louis we are working on a program which will prepare experienced public school teachers to go out and work with the schools of the slums, to equip these people to meet and surmount the problems they will face there. May we not do the same with those just now preparing to be teachers, with those in other disciplines? May we not do more of this in medicine and the health sciences, through special "mission" clinics; in social welfare, through actual on-the-job training; in sociology; in health, physical education and recreation? Could we not send our students in the performing arts to present neighborhood or street corner concerts and art shows; or our English majors and budding novelists to man language and literacy clinics? Could we not thus inject a note of "evangelism" into education, taking hope directly to the slums? The President of New York University has said that the urban university by virtue of its location encourages "engagement with the realities of life." Perhaps we should make this a more active part of our philosophy in all facets of education—so that we and our students may learn while bringing the glimmer of learning to those in trouble.

5. Conversely, we might consider bringing the underprivileged to us. In St. Louis, there is currently a small movement in which underprivileged school children go as a group to the most distinguished restaurants in the city and there have lunch. The thought behind this is that, despite the education a person may receive, he may still feel "out-of-place" or actually be afraid to enter places in a city with which he is not familiar. Could we not extend this concept to our urban universities by having young members of the underprivileged groups attend events on our campuses, to teach them to be familiar with a university atmosphere so that they may aspire to take advantage of educational opportunity. This could be extended to an active "crash" program with older and younger

endure as we know it on the teetering foundation of smouldering trouble in our urban communities.

This is our lesson and our challenge.

I am confident that the 21st Century will look back to see that we learned our lesson well—that our urban universities were equal to the challenges facing them—that we made our cities our joys once again and by so doing made our whole world a better one.

*Delivered at the 19th National Conference on Higher Education, Association for Higher Education, Chicago, Illinois, April 20, 1964.*

# 10

# The Price of Excellence

In 1954, Walter Lippmann sounded a tocsin that commanded nationwide attention. He talked on "The Shortage in Education," and in part he said:

> Our educational effort has not been raised to the plateau of the age we live in. . . . We must measure our educational effort as we do our military effort. That is to say, we must measure it not by what it would be easy and convenient to do, but by what it is necessary to do in order that the nation may survive and flourish. We have learned that we are quite rich enough to defend ourselves, whatever the cost. We must now learn that we are quite rich enough to educate ourselves as we need to be educated.[1]

The voluntary aid-to-education movement has accelerated a good deal since 1954. In a biennial survey completed by the Council for Financial Aid to Education, of support of America's colleges and universities during 1964–65, a record $1,245,000,000 was reported by the institutions that took part —$333 million more than the grand total of the 1962–63 survey. It looks as if the projected need of $2 billion in voluntary support, by 1969–70, should be an achievable goal, especially if you extrapolate the total reported in 1964–65 to $1,556,-000,000 for the "whole universe" of America's higher educational establishment.

The grim fact, however, is that, compared with the future pace that will be required of the "private sector" in helping to finance American higher education, all that we have witnessed so far has been pedestrian.

It is now clear that our colleges and universities have been running much harder than ever before, only to maintain the same relative position as to needs versus support. We have been observing what the Germans call *Eine Besserung zum Schlechtem,* an improvement for the worse. Everything has become bigger in scale than anything we have known previously: student enrollments, faculty compensation (still far from high enough), costs of brick and mortar, and especially expenditures for the educational program. The more the universities do, the more the nation calls upon them to do. I cite only one instance: the vast demand from virtually all segments of our national economy for more graduates of our professional and graduate schools. Providing for expanded graduate education reaches deeply into the universities' operating income, which seldom is adequate.

Here are some of the outlines of this growing problem. In the period 1953–1963 undergraduate enrollment in America's colleges and universities increased by 99 per cent; graduate enrollment, by 117 per cent. The U.S. Office of Education has estimated that the increases in the period 1963–1973 will be 65 per cent for undergraduate and 78 per cent for graduate enrollment.

In actual count, during the last few years, the numbers enrolled in the graduate and professional schools at the University of Michigan, for example, have passed the undergraduate enrollment. In 1963–64 the comparable numbers were 3,498 bachelor's degrees and 3,642 graduate degrees.

Michigan, in a statement about its proposed 1966–67 budget said this to the legislature: "Because Michigan has a large enrollment of graduate and graduate-professional students, such as those in medicine, dentistry, law, public health, and social work, its total cost of instruction is much higher than if all its students were undergraduates." The University gave the cost per credit hour of instruction as follows:

| | |
|---|---|
| Freshman-sophomore | $ 47.19 |
| Junior-senior | 62.58 |
| Master's degree | 95.95 |
| Doctor of philosophy | 205.75 |
| Graduate-professional | 85.27 |

The average costs are: undergraduate, $54.88 an hour; and graduate, $128.99 an hour.

Such sobering facts make it clear that, while voluntary support has been growing in volume, the demands on American institutions of higher learning have been growing still faster. In the autumn of 1965 the Council for Financial Aid to Education, on a test-run basis, asked fourteen college and university presidents whether, in relation to current educational programs, they thought their institutions were better off financially than they were in 1954; or in about the same status, or worse off. The note common to most of the replies was sounded in this comment from a heavily endowed eastern university:

> In brief, my point is that although we may appear to be better off financially in some respects, a great deal more is being demanded of us. On top of this is the quantitative pressure of the increased number of students. My own bet is that we are worse off than we were ten years ago.

Despite this somber set of facts, I am inclined to be optimistic about the future of voluntary support. If people know the price for excellence they will pay it.

The potential for meeting that price is indicated by a number of important aspects of the Council for Financial Aid to Education 1964–65 survey. General welfare foundations contributed to the participating colleges and universities a record total of $357,600,709, the largest amount contributed in any CFAE survey year by any source. The 1964–65 grants from the foundations were $145 million more than the 1962–63 comparable figures.

Non-alumni individuals, those hard-to-identify but potential friends of higher education, contributed the second largest amount to the colleges and universities: $309,692,143. This group became the second source to top the $300 million mark since the CFAE initiated the biennial survey of voluntary support in 1954–55.

But the alumni, for reasons hard to fathom, fell from first place in 1962–63 to third place in 1964–65. Their contributions in 1964–65 amounted to $248,401,446. The rate of growth of alumni gifts since 1962–63 was 12.4 per cent, as compared with 68 per cent for foundations and 57 per cent for non-alumni individuals.

As in all previous Council surveys, business corporations in 1964–65 stood fourth among the various sources of voluntary support. They contributed $173,985,935. The companies' contributions increased by 18.6 per cent over their 1962–63 total, but represented only 14 per cent of the 1964–65 grand total. The comparable figure for 1962–63 was 16.1 per cent, and in 1960–61 it was 16.3 per cent.

Now what do all these figures boil down to? Several things are obvious. In the first place, alumni ought to be a much larger source of support than they are for the colleges and universities. Of the eight groups of institutions, only the private women's colleges and the private men's colleges received more during 1964–65 from their alumni(ae) than from any other source.

In the second place, I believe that the potential of corporate support is far above its present level. As far back as 1951 this source was described, in an article in *The New York Sunday Times Magazine,* as a "New Giant in Giving," and as the last untapped source of voluntary support for higher education. One reason the New Giant is today fourth in batting averages is that, by and large, the colleges do not throw him the right kind of pitches. Recently the Opinion Research Corporation conducted a study for the Cleveland Commission on Higher Education to obtain an accurate evaluation of corporate opinion, attitudes and commitments in support of higher education; the extent and depth of this involvement and knowledge of the higher educational enterprise; their present plans, and methods of handling appeals.

A few of the salient findings will be of interest to you:

1. One in eight of both Light and Heavy Contributors indicate that their future direction in emphasis will be determined by the action of the federal government, but heavy contributors are almost unanimous in rejecting the idea that such government activity undermines the need for corporate support to education.

2. Appraising education's future needs, executives put strengthening college faculties first. This is pivotal—far more important than plant and equipment.

3. Principal demand is for explicit financial reports—how much money comes from business and the other sources, how the money is spent. Also, what are the unfilled needs and the projected costs.

4. Less than half of the Cleveland company executives feel that the typical appeal is realistically geared to the businessman's thinking, "They don't know how to sell. They talk about their needs, not ours."

5. Only one of the five college members of the CCHE is credited with doing an outstanding job of soliciting.

6. There is marked resistance to any set formula for contributing to education.

I should like to conclude by commenting on the basic worries which are haunting educators but especially those responsible for private colleges and universities, with the exception of the relatively few which are financially stable.

The critical situation today represents a conflict between two national objectives. One new and laudable objective is, in its implementation, rendering another older objective incapable of achievement. The more recent objective is free post-high-school education for all qualified American youth. The older objective is a strong dual system of public and private higher education in America. To achieve the former, new tax-supported junior colleges, community colleges, and universities are being established at a fantastic rate, while the existing public institutions continue to bulge with increasing enrollments. In the meantime, most private colleges and universities, still relying for subsistence on income from tuition and the support of alumni, business corporations, and that occasional but wildly welcome five- or six-figure gift from a wealthy friend, are finding themselves incapable of attracting either excellent faculty or the better students in competition with the expanding operational and capital budgets of their tax-supported brethren. If the present trend continues, about fifteen years from now, only twenty per cent of college teachers and students will be found in private institutions, and, because of financial anemia, this segment of both faculty and students will, on the whole, not compare favorably with their counterparts in the public sector. If I read the signs of the times accurately, private colleges are headed for the same fate that has been suffered by the small-town merchant, the regional telephone company, and the second-line automobile producer. In education as well as in business, the near-monopolist can 'manufacture' his product at greatly reduced costs thus forcing his competitor either to become equally powerful (and most can't) or to go out of business. If the latter alternative becomes the unwilling choice of much of private higher education, the older American objective—a balanced and strong public-private higher educational system—although once hailed as the chief bulwark of academic freedom and flexibility, will be relegated to the archives of earlier American history.

On the other hand, let us assume that this trend is worth stopping or at least slowing down. What would have to happen? The American people, through their representatives in many facets of our society, would have to do a number of things. The list of musts is lengthy, and probably all or nearly all of them would be required to do the job, not just one or two.

a) Community and state colleges and public universities would have to prove their sincere desire for strong private institutions by continuing to increase their tuition rates *at least slightly*, so that the gap between their costs and those of private institutions does not become increasingly larger.

b) State legislatures would have to demonstrate their belief in the dual system by providing state scholarships for a substantial number of qualified but financially handicapped students to attend a college of their choice within the state. Fourteen states already have adopted such measures. Eventually, a tuition grant program such as that in New York and Wisconsin should be extended throughout the country.

c) The Federal Government must exercise leadership in fostering private as well as public higher education by including among its rapidly multiplying forms of aid such programs as are explicitly designed to strengthen the smaller and particularly the private institution which desperately needs general funds to attract and retain a competent faculty, not categorical grants for specialized purposes.

d) The foundations, in addition to or in lieu of some of their highly specialized types of support, should also do their share to stem the tide which is threatening the private sector by initiating imaginative programs aimed at injecting the lifeblood of operational stability into undernourished institutions.

e) The Churches should either give substantial continuing support to their colleges because they, too, are convinced of the importance of a balanced educational system, or they should break off their present unmerited and often inhibiting relationship to permit these colleges to make their way as private non-denominational institutions.

f) Alumni, corporations, and friends should increase their annual unrestricted giving to higher education, especially to private colleges, because along with the rest of the American public they are dedicated to the long-standing objective of a healthy public-private system. Here much of the burden falls on the private colleges themselves, most of whom have not done a creditable job in building up an organized and continuing development and public relations program.

In the list of musts above are measures which will undoubtedly be considered revolutionary, but this situation calls for drastically innovative departures. Nothing short of such deliberate, pin-pointed efforts as described above will achieve what John Gardner has listed as one of the important 'Agenda' of today—to bring the smaller colleges in America back into the mainstream of our intellectual life. Our society's newer objective of free post-high-school education for all may be sound, but even so, its eventual achievement should not be sought at the price of sacrificing another extremely sound objective—a vigorous public-private system of higher education—something which many others besides myself still believe is one of our country's most precious possessions.

The greater the demand for higher education, naturally, the greater the cost of the establishment. America today looks to its colleges and universities both for quantitative service and more and more excellence. All of us in business know that quality is expensive. We know also that the public will buy it. Everyone in business and industry ought, I think, to realize that academic excellence is expensive. Everyone ought to comprehend as well that the bill for it has to be paid, and that the nation can well afford to pay it. At a time in our history when we as a nation have to be strong at all points, we need to put more money into the strongest safe deposit box of them all, our intellectual bank. And the time scheme of things gives us no quarter. We have to act *now*, and act adequately.

*Delivered before a business executives' meeting, sponsored by the Council for Financial Aid to Education, May 1966.*

## NOTE

1. Walter Lippmann, "The Shortage in Education," *Atlantic Monthly*, May 1954, p. 38.

# 11

# Student Unrest

If you've been watching Walter Cronkite lately, you probably have noticed the increasing use of battle maps to indicate where the major engagements are taking place. I should mention that I'm not referring to Viet Nam, but a map of the United States. And the names on the map are not those of cities, but of universities. One night recently, there were a dozen campuses pin-pointed on the map.

I am sure you are deeply concerned about campus unrest. But not any more than I am. As one wag commented: "Who says mothers don't worry about their sons away at school? Have you talked to the mother of a college president recently?"

My remarks today are somewhat different from the talk I had written several weeks ago and had originally planned to give. I was going to explain to you how St. Louis University had managed to avoid any episodes of campus unrest. Then, on April 28, we became one of the pins on the national map. A dozen members of the Association of Black Collegians occupied a dean's office for eleven hours.

The theme of my original remarks, however, seems even more relevant than before the sit-in. As you will see, my talk emphasizes the importance of open channels of communication. And the necessity for that was never made more clear to me than it was three weeks ago.

St. Louis University had prided itself on the fact that each administrator, faculty member and student was concerned about each other's viewpoint and problems and ready to discuss them. Yet when our channels of communication became temporarily blocked—or, at least, seemed to be blocked—we had our first confrontation.

Still, we were able to end it before the day was over, without any violence or damage, without any real disruption of campus life, and, more positively, with an even greater climate of understanding and cooperation. The students had some justifiable and urgent grievances, intimately related to their life on a campus that is 97 per cent white, and we were able to sit down with them, in an atmosphere of mutual respect and cordiality, and discuss matters. Everybody on the campus gained from the experience. But the whole incident emphasized very dramatically what can happen when there is even a temporary breakdown in communications. And I believe that is what the current wave of campus disorders is all about. On those campuses where internal communications closely resemble a case of hardening of the arteries, the campus has been literally torn apart.

I want to make clear that I do not condone disruptive activity on any campus. If the students on our own campus had caused any violence or damaged any property—or if there were any indications that they planned to—or if their grievances had not been reasonable and in line with requests that we had been discussing for months, or if they seemed bent on disruption for disruption's sake, I would have invoked our policy governing such situations, and have ordered the campus police to remove them. But that was not the case.

Also, the consequences of calling in the police could have been very serious. The campus of St. Louis University is located on the edge of the ghetto, and the city police were concerned that any effort to remove the students could very easily ignite violence in the surrounding community. We chose to allow a dean's office to be closed for half a day, rather than have the entire university shut down indefinitely. We chose to talk, rather than use force. It seems ironic that those who criticized us for not using violent means during the crisis are the very ones who deplore the violence they have seen on other campuses.

Over the past few years, I have studied the problem of student unrest quite extensively, and discussed it a number of times, on platforms ranging from the Advanced Administrative Institute at Harvard University last summer to a national conference on our own campus last month. It would be foolhardy to claim that I have all the answers or even some of them, but at least I may have some insights that are relevant to any discussion of the relationships of education, business, and our urban society. After all, the youth of today are not only our students, but your future employees and customers and the citizens of urban America; they are the ones who will determine the environment in which your company operates.

The youth of today have been badly maligned, for in general they are bright, concerned, responsible, sensitive, highly capable, very endearing people, more eager than any generation that preceded them to make our society better. Their "corporate image" is bad because of a very small percentage of their numbers who are anarchists in the true sense of the word, determined to destroy our society without any plans to replace the rubble. These students are able to influence enough of their classmates to make any sit-in or demonstration look like an outpouring of student sentiment. What is not seen on the television screen is the vast majority of students who are going about their business in pursuit of an education and who regard these disruptions of campus life as an infringement on their own rights as students.

I believe the reason for the relative stability of campus life at St. Louis University is related to the fact that our students have channeled their concern for the improvement of society into constructive activity. Our students represent the largest single source of volunteer help for the inner-city programs of the city of St. Louis. I'd like to mention just a few of these projects. During the past year, for example, our students rented and renovated four different tenement houses in the ghetto areas and turned them into tutoring centers for underprivileged children. More than twenty fraternities, sororities and other campus organizations held a Christmas drive and collected food, toys and clothing for some three hundred needy families in the area of the University. They raised more than $2,000 for food shipments to the starving people of Biafra. They held picnics for orphans, organized a basketball league for inner-city grade school children, took them to Halloween and Christmas parties, painted a downtown school, worked with our Department of Education in establishing a course on teaching the culturally disadvantaged, served as teachers, counselors and nurses in dozens of parishes, schools and hospitals. They did all this without pay, without academic credit, and without any desire for public recognition.

The same kind of projects are being pursued on other campuses throughout the country, but unfortunately they do not often appear on your television screen or in your newspapers.

In twenty years as a university president, I have known two generations of college students. The first class to which I handed degrees in 1949 was part of what is now called the "Silent Generation." Maybe that includes some of you here today. That class was proud of what it had done to preserve freedom from fascism, determined to rebuild their personal lives and realize hibernating ambitions. But it would have been a real oddity to find a member of that class working without pay as a volunteer in an inner-city program. And certainly the slums were just as bad then as they are now.

That is one major difference between the class of 1949 and the class of 1969. Another may be that the class of 1949 had already found a spiritual cause and was ready to turn to more material goals. The class of today, on the other hand, has already experienced the realization of material goals and is hungry for a spiritual cause.

While the class of 1949 has been called the "silent generation," I prefer to call the class of 1969 the "unlistened-to generation." At least, they seem to be unlistened to until they reach college campuses, and then they demand an audience. Maybe it has something to do with the pace of life while they were children, the preoccupation of their parents with "making a living." Maybe it has something to do with the television set which, in many homes, has assumed a surrogate role as teacher-counselor. Incidentally, one of our history professors recently suggested that television also has played a role in making our students so impatient to solve the problems of society of their own universities. He noted that today's students have been raised on a diet of television programs like "Mission:Impossible" in which each problem is solved in a single hour. The previous generation, on the other hand, was exposed to the continuing radio or movie serial, whose success depended upon how long a problem could be extended.

The need of today's students for a receptive ear is evident, as I indicated before, when you consider that those campuses that have been rocked by student unrest have had what Motorola might call trouble on the network. Those campuses that have been relatively peaceful have had open channels of communication, with every segment of the campus community ready to listen to every other.

At the root of the students' need to be heard are some basic frustrations—frustration over Viet Nam; frustration over the inequities of the Selective Service System; frustration with the quality of teaching he is receiving, in many cases from a graduate assistant replacing a professor who prefers to spend his time in the research laboratory; frustration with the slow progress of efforts to achieve social justice, and frustration over the de-humanization of society.

Almost all students feel these frustrations; many seek to relieve them through constructive work in the ghettos and in projects such as the Peace Corps; a small handful seek to relieve them through violent confrontation. In most cases what they want to attack is the military-industrial complex and the nearest target is their own campus which they consider an embodiment and energizer of that intangible complex. As you may have noticed, I have no use for students who use violent outlets for these frustrations.

At the same time, I do sympathize with them in their concern over the problems of contemporary society. They are given the best education this country has ever offered. And all they can look forward to on graduation is not a career in their chosen field or post-graduate education in professional or graduate schools, but boredom, injury and even death in the jungles and rice paddies of a far-off land in a war that, according to all of the polls, nobody wants. They are taught that all men are created equal and they do not find this concept alive in our society. They are highly trained in science and technology, but react against the evils that our technological society has wrought upon our environment. Finally they react to frustrations on their own campuses.

Last month students at St. Louis University sponsored a conference entitled "Toward an Understanding of Campus Community" and it brought together students, faculty and administrators of some twenty colleges and universities across the country to discuss, without benefit of picket signs and sit-ins, what could be done to heal the divisions so evident on campuses around the country. This conference was planned

as a contribution to our 150th anniversary, but I believe that
the result of it may be an even greater contribution to higher
education in the United States. The final report points out that

> within the present style of campus living it would appear
> that each of the three constituent groups watch the other
> two, generally with suspicious and distrustful eyes. For ex-
> ample, the students are reported to see the faculty as inter-
> ested only in rank and tenure for material advancement;
> exercising no leadership role and lax in criticizing the estab-
> lished order, concentrating on research while the students
> focus concern on contemporary problems; seeing academic
> freedom as their exclusive prerogative, to be jealously and
> reluctantly shared; prima donnas trained through graduate
> schools to be specialists and to be prosperous but possessed
> of very narrow views. The response by faculty to such
> charges is often that teachers are bound by institutional sys-
> tems of rewards which make such behavior almost inevitable.
> Students want a man primarily concerned with relevant
> teaching done through person-to-person encounter both
> within and outside the classroom. But time spent with stu-
> dents outside the classroom is not rewarded, time devoted to
> scholarly research is. A faculty member's reputation is estab-
> lished not so much by habitual brilliant teaching perform-
> ance on his campus, but through recognition by the scholars
> in his discipline. Such recognition is achieved through
> scholarly research and publication.[1]

The report asks: "What do students want?" And answers:
"An end to confrontation, a switch to communication and cooperation, honesty and frankness from administrators, recognition that students have something to contribute and are
integral and accepted members of the campus community."
I agree entirely with that summation, and at the risk of
referring too often to my own university, I should point out
that we are one of only two universities that I know of who
have added students to their highest deliberative body and
are now adding them to almost all of our committees. This
was not done under duress but out of a conviction that stu-

dents do have something to offer in the operation of the University.

I am convinced that if a number of other universities had recognized this earlier they would not have been in the headlines. But universities by tradition have not been democratic institutions; rather they have been among the most authoritarian institutions in our society, and they will not change overnight.

Neither will they change overnight to meet the problems of our urban society. Leonard J. Duhl, chief of the Planning Staff of the National Institute of Mental Health, sees the university as "the most important agent in promoting change in our society. Though it no longer has a monopoly on ideas or education, it has a history and a tradition which make all the more important its active participation in urban society. Its role as the social critic and the conscience of our society must be continued into the future. As a dominant change agent it must educate those people, do that kind of scholarly work, give that kind of consultation, which will move us closer to the good life. The values, the ideals, the spirit that we associate with the best universities must be maintained, and the institutions must reach out to all segments of our society that deal with people."[2]

At the same time he points out that "most universities have become involved in the urban scene simply by being there— being in the middle of a slum, requiring space, responding to the role of urban renewal agents, of landlords, of protector of faculty and administrative staff. How many universities were not aware of the community until a secretary was mugged or a professor beaten? How many ignore the problems of planning and zoning until new dormitories or new classrooms have to be built? How many became concerned only when offstreet parking space grew critically short and student commuters complained?"[3]

Charles Lazarus, president of the F. and R. Lazarus Company, of Columbus, Ohio, in a talk before the American Association of Collegiate Schools of Business emphasized the tardiness of our universities in meeting urban problems. He said he thumbed through the faculty and staff directory at his own university, Ohio State, and counted more than 300 full-time people who represented agricultural interests, but only ten who had even a remote connection with urban problems.

Many universities, including my own, are trying to make up for lost time with the establishment last year of our Center for Urban Programs.

Within the university, faculty and administrators will continue to debate whether or not urban studies and involvement are legitimate functions of the university. I am convinced that they are and that the debate only delays that confrontation with them. After all, our universities were responsible to a great extent for creating our urban society, with all its technological and social problems, so it would seem that they have a responsibility for the quality of life there.

If the universities, particularly the urban universities, have been slow in recognizing and meeting the challenges of urban problems, the business community has been setting the same pace.

And I believe that the reluctance of the business community to become involved in problems of the larger community may be one reason that companies find it increasingly difficult to recruit college graduates. As part of a national survey conducted by the American Council on Education, we surveyed our freshmen class last fall and one thing that the survey revealed was that business was the second most popular career choice of these freshmen students. But I think it's safe to predict that it will not be the second most popular choice upon their graduation because during their collegiate careers they become increasingly idealistic and concerned with problems of society and do not find an outlet for that concern in a business career.

Last year a professor at Indiana University conducted a survey of graduates with master's degrees in business administration to learn the extent of their own and their companies' understanding and participation in community affairs. These were men who received their degrees within the last eight years and who now hold executive jobs in junior and middle management. He found that one out of three of these rising young executives participates in his community in no way whatsoever. Participation of the other two is virtually limited to fund-raising for the United Appeal or, as we call it in St. Louis, the United Fund; for churches, and thank God, for universities. I do not want to denigrate this kind of participation, but it is certainly not central to the basic problems of the urban community. Again, only three out of ten respondents felt that their company considered it essential for an executive to participate in community affairs. Two-thirds reported that they had received no training at all in graduate school to help them participate effectively in the community. Many said that they were concerned about community problems, but found only frustration in attempting to confront them in the corporate environment. Some pointed out that they were frustrated by their company's own dictum that profit is the only legitimate corporate goal. If this is the attitude of M.B.A. graduates, who are intent on business careers, you can readily see why undergraduates are not crowding the personnel offices, for they certainly do not consider profit as the only legitimate corporate goal or the only goal of their lives.

Education and business have worked closely together to build our highly productive society. I believe that they have a new opportunity to forge a unique partnership in meeting the social problems of that society. There are already some beginnings.

I believe a good example of what can be done is contained in a booklet recently published by the Department of Labor that sets out guidelines for operating effective summer youth employment programs. This booklet was produced by the

Center for Urban Programs at St. Louis University in cooperation with a number of groups, including the St. Louis unit of
the National Alliance of Businessmen and Civic Progress, Incorporated, which is composed of many of the top business
executives in the city. The Center studied the youth employment program in St. Louis in the summer of 1968, in which
these groups participated, and established a model for other
cities. The result is a booklet that has been adopted nationally
by the Department of Labor, the National Alliance of Businessmen, and the President's Council.

The real need is for a serious recognition by both the corporate community and the educational community that the
problems of the urban society are their own problems and that
if they don't join together to solve them no one else will. In
doing so, they will give hope and encouragement to the young
people who are their students, their future employees, customers, future citizens of this country. This will not be an
easy task, for we are faced with twin revolutions—on the one
hand, a revolution in the personal aspirations of people
throughout our society, particularly minority groups, a demand for their birthright, a realization of the American dream
of equality of opportunity, of personal dignity and fulfillment.
This revolution is confronted by another, an increasingly specialized economy. In the words of Chancellor Gould at the
State University of New York, "The time-honored Horatio
Alger dream of success through pluck and luck and determination is becoming obsolete. High professional competence
and esoteric skills are rapidly becoming the essential keys to
upper mobility. For the first time in man's history, the unskilled worker is largely obsolete."

This is just one of the dilemmas that education and business
must solve together. As I have indicated, there are many
others. But the possibility of this strong and powerful partnership holds promise for the future of every American. Every
company and every college should be involved. We must

enter this partnership with a firm conviction that what is good for the people of this country, for every citizen, is good for them, too.

Again let me quote Mr. Lazarus:

> None of us likes to tell a stockholder that profits depend on something more than how we run the business. In consequence, many of us pretend our companies are little islands —saved from the winds of social and civil upheaval. And yet you and I know that no corporation can earn a predictable profit in years to come unless we meet the present rebellion with workable answers. And I don't mean answers acceptable only to the corporation, but answers that can be endorsed by the whole community.

> To put it bluntly, when riots occur, business comes to a shuddering halt. Customers stay home. Buses don't run. Employees can't get to work. Our physical plant is endangered. Police costs mount. Taxes go up. The impact of riots on the balance sheet can be enormous. Am I justified in trying to help Columbus, Ohio, do those things that will improve its business climate and environment? I think I am.[4]

So are St. Louis University and Motorola. But I hope my remarks suggest to you that our commitment goes far beyond the balance sheet and the diploma.

*Given at the Motorola Executive Institute, Vail, Arizona, May 15, 1969.*


## NOTES

1. Richard Fortin, ed., *Toward an Understanding of Campus Community* (Saint Louis University, 1969).

2. Leonard J. Duhl, "The University and the Urban Condition," *The Educational Record* (Washington, D.C.: American Council on Education, Summer 1965, pp. 332–33.

3. *Ibid.*

4. Charles Lazarus. Address before the American Association of Collegiate Schools of Business, 1969.

# 12

## Modernizing Mark Hopkins

Back in 1871 James A. Garfield, onetime professor of classical languages and, later, President of the United States, was addressing the alumni of Williams College. "Give me a log hut," he said, "with only a simple bench, Mark Hopkins on one end and I on the other, and you may have all the buildings, apparatus, and libraries without him." In other words, Garfield was emphasizing that the essential function of education consists solely in establishing a relationship between a great teacher like Mark Hopkins on one end of a log bench and a typical student like himself on the other. Nearly a century later, this process of teaching and learning, in keeping with most facets of American life, has exchanged beautiful simplicity for what often seems chaotic complexity. Today the teacher Mark Hopkins has been replaced by thousands of professors in a hundred different specialized departments; James Garfield, the student, has been multiplied into institutional enrollments numbering ten, twenty, even thirty thousand; the log bench on which they sat has grown into magnificent laboratories, libraries, student unions and dormitories; and this whole bewildering process of bringing teacher and student together has become one of the most expensive undertakings that either government or private philanthropy has ever tried to support.

The most fundamental point which I think needs emphasis as we begin this conference is that no matter how complex the apparatus of higher education may become, we cannot dare to lose sight of the essential nature of the learning process. What is that? The stimulation of a young mind by a wiser one to pursue and explore and embrace truth. The primary mission of a college or university is to provide the ideal environment in which a human being may be motivated to reach the highest level of maturity through the acquisition of knowledge and wisdom. Insofar as we educators contribute to creating and maintaining that environment we are a success; insofar as we hinder or violate that environment we are a failure, whether we are administrators, teachers, public relations men or development officers.

Fundamentally, what is happening today is that communication from the universities to the public and from the public to the universities has been intensified. Our stake in keeping the public correctly informed is much clearer to us than ever before. I can exemplify most tangibly what is happening by pointing to my own institution—a medium-sized independent university—where in the last seven years alone we have brought together functions which in 1950 required the services of only two men and two stenographers, and have combined them into an administrative area with six executives, three professional staff members and eight stenographers under the direction of a vice-president. I am endeavoring to make only one point: that the task we all now recognize as essential,

namely, a two-way flow of information between higher education and its public, has led to the creation of a new area of
educational administration and to a unique kind of educational
officer who obviously must possess far-reaching responsibility
and commensurate authority.

It is this expanding function of development and public
relations which has led to this conference devoted to a study
of management functions separately and the problem of
grouping these functions into a sound organizational pattern.
I assume that one reason why a study of this kind, though so
obviously needed, has taken so long to materialize is that the
two organizations most logically concerned, ACPRA and
AAC, have shied away from the subject for fear of treading
on each other's territory. Their hesitancy about trespassing
has now been recognized, I think, as a disservice to their
members and to higher education. It is much to the credit of
both organizations that they have made this very significant
cooperative attack on such a pressing problem.

## The "Professional Soldier" Theory

One of our most fundamental tasks is to explode within our
own academic walls what I like to call the "professional
soldier" theory of development and public relations. According to this theory, if your college decides it needs money or
wants to "improve its public relations," you go out and find
an expert and add him to your full-time staff, or you retain
professional counsel, or both. Then the rest of the institution
sits back and waits for results. Very few college or university
presidents would subscribe to this absurd extreme, but there
are large numbers of faculty and academic administrators who
do not comprehend the essence of the development-public-
relations function. As I see it, your work is not a process of
doing something in place of them so that the faculty and
academic administration can argue that the "professional" is
doing the development-public-relations job for them. Rather

your task is the process of bringing them together with the public, whether that public be students, alumni, business, legislatures, trustees, or what have you.

The only method by which we can explode the "professional soldier" theory is to convince the individual college teacher that he is the key development-public-relations person.

Your function is that of "bringing together," not of substituting for the faculty in its relationship to the public. This function is easiest to understand when it is intended to create immediate direct results—a gift, for example. But more often this "bringing together" of faculty and public is needed to contribute to a proper understanding or even to an awareness of the institution. In spite of all the efforts expended, the lack of public knowledge about the typical college or university is absolutely unbelievable.

On the one hand, therefore, it is abundantly clear that we still have a long way to go in accomplishing the primary function of public relations and development, that of "bringing together" our faculty and our institution with its many publics. On the other, the key problem in trying to achieve this objective is dispelling from the minds of the academicians the false assumption that the "professional P.R. soldiers" are solely responsible for this job. The first problem is this: How do you convince the faculty that you do not do the public-relations-development job, but that the best you can do is to help them get the job done?

## The Over-Simplified "Communications" Theory

There is a second serious problem to be faced, a second theory to be exploded, and one which is closely related to the first theory just discussed. Not only must the professors and deans be aware of their direct role in public relations and development, but we must also bring everyone to the realization that the key to understanding on the part of our publics is involvement, not merely the over-simplified notion of communications. Lay appreciation of the educational process will never be achieved without involving them in the process. Neither stepping up the number of news releases nor resorting to the latest communications techniques will by themselves achieve public understanding. Nothing short of direct participation and involvement will suffice.

And let's not minimize the difficulty of putting the principle of involvement into practice. It can be a very painful process. First of all, our publics—alumni, businessmen—are engrossed in a multiplicity of problems of their own, and understandably they resist any effort to involve them to the extent of devoting time and effort to our cause. Secondly, if they suspect that involvement is really aimed only at getting them to give money themselves or getting others to give, the resistance is intensified. Thirdly, active, continuing participation of the public in educational matters other than fund raising bristles with all sorts of thorny problems. For example, if you do not give participating groups all of the most intimate facts about your institution, you may be judged guilty of deceit and insincerity. On the other hand, open access to everything in the institution can sometimes lead to outside control and to conflicts on academic, professional policies which certainly are the prerogative of the faculty and the institutional administrators. Again, lay participation cannot endure unless it is a two-way process in which the faculty is also willing to give of its time and effort to make such participation stimulating and profitable. Yet, in spite of these and hundreds of other difficulties, there is no other way in which public understanding can be achieved except through various forms of continuing lay participation.

In promoting such participation, your role as a public relations-development officer is again a unique and difficult one. The teacher's task in the classroom is reasonably self-contained; he is sufficient unto himself. Give an engineer some iron and he can build a bridge. Give a surgeon a scalpel and a man with an infected appendix and he can perform an operation. These men are all important for what they can do; you are not valuable for what you do so much as for what you can get others to do. Your job is not self-contained; the effectiveness of your accomplishment lies outside yourself. It means getting the internal faculty and academic administrators involved in continuing participation with the external publics with a view to establishing mutual understanding.

### Qualifications of a Public-Relations-Development Officer

Now if you are not already hopelessly discouraged by the unique difficulties which I think are identified with your position, I would like to conclude briefly with a listing of some of the most important qualities which I think you must possess to meet the demands implied.

1) We assume that you possess the professional techniques which can give us the services we need: writing and communications skills, organizational abilities, knowledge of the community. The program which you must help to conduct should produce benefits far more comprehensive than newspaper print and greenbacks. The tricks of your trade are a very important but only a small portion of what must go into the making of a successful public-relations-development officer.

2) You must acquire a deep, genuine understanding of the educational process, above all, of its ultimate purposes. To understand education, one must understand Mark Hopkins; understand that, though there are exceptions as in all professions, the college teacher is basically a person extraordinarily devoted and dedicated to learning. Typically, he loves wisdom and knowledge for its own intrinsic value, and hence he is congenitally allergic to associating learning with materialistic concepts—money, glamor, publicity. To him, the introduction of commercial "selling" techniques into the educational process is the worst kind of prostitution. Let me

emphasize that I am not arguing that the attitudes of college professors in these and other matters are always above reproach—far from it. But here is a situation which you as a member of the college or university team must recognize as a fact to be reckoned with as you work with each Mark Hopkins on your campus.

3) Not only must you understand the educational process and profession thoroughly; you must know perfectly the special problems in your own institution. If you move from one to another, the worst mistake possible would be to assume that the problems in the second college are about the same as in the first. In my experience, the academic officers—deans, directors of departments, and all who are responsible for educational policy—harbor two basic fears about you people. First, they are afraid that you will misrepresent the institution because you really have only a very superficial knowledge of what is going on. Second, they are apprehensive that in order to achieve your purposes, however legitimate, you are dedicated to changing the essential educational operations within the institution. There have been just enough blunders on the part of some of your brethren to give credence to these fears.

4) You must be willing to be admitted to membership in the educational family on the basis of merit, not by reason of title or by executive legislation. A first-year instructor does not expect to be appointed to faculty committees charged with far-reaching policy decisions. Likewise, the public relations or development officer should be given open access to whatever information he needs immediately to do effective work, but he can earn the right to participate in important educational discussion and decision only through a capacity for policy-making that has been demonstrated by his interest, understanding, loyalty, and lengthy service.

5) In describing the unique difficulties of your position earlier, I said that it is not so much what you do as what you get others to do that is important. One of the qualities necessary for success, however, is the ability not to misunderstand

or abuse this principle. It is true that the essential activities in public relations and development must be done by the faculty and the lay public. But this does not mean that there are not many very important things which you alone must do. Yours is the behind-the-scene task of providing the services which the faculty and the volunteer participant have neither time nor skill to perform themselves. You all know the work I am referring to: from typing, listing, furnishing information, and making appointments to much more important jobs such as stimulating ideas. The faculty particularly must become convinced from your day-to-day attitude that you are really dedicated to working for them. Instead I have seen the idea get abroad among the faculty—with some justification—that the job of the public relations man is to think up more work for already overburdened teachers. Service to the essential actors in the drama of public relations and development is essential.

6) As I list the qualities I consider crucial for your success, may I exhort you to cultivate unbounded patience and humility. Public relations and development in the college and university world is still a very young idea. The average college teacher, dean, or president can be expected to accept only so much of you and your ideas on faith. The rest must wait for and depend on actual performance. The old adage has never had a truer application than in this field: "Nothing succeeds like success." You must be willing, therefore, to move ahead slowly and constructively. If you want recognition, you'll never get it by worrying because your efforts are going unnoticed. Keep remembering what Ralph Waldo Emerson said: "There is no limit to what can be accomplished if it doesn't matter who gets the credit." Boisterous condemnation of the lack of understanding and enthusiasm on the part of the benighted faculty, maybe even of the administration, will only end in disaster and the tragedy of starting all over again. So pray for patience and humility.

7) Finally, as a public relations or development officer in

a college or university, remember that you are essentially a unique kind of salesman for higher education. The world is full of salesmen, some of them so unscrupulous they would convince an Eskimo in our forty-ninth state he needs a refrigerator; others are peddling worthless products to unsuspecting, gullible victims. But you must be a salesman or saleswoman of professional integrity. You are selling a genuine quality product, one of the most valuable possessions in the world—human wisdom. Yours should be the same dedication, the same spiritual motivation as that of Mark Hopkins and all great teachers. And this moral integrity is not something you can put on outside your real self like an academic cap and gown. No, it must be part of your very inner being. The financial support, the future students, the public understanding you are seeking for your institution—all these and much else will be forthcoming only if it is obvious that you are motivated by the conviction that, nurturing within yourself the precious possession of human wisdom and moral integrity, you are driven on with a fierce desire to share this pearl of great price with others. Only this sincerely genuine motivation will keep you on the job, determined to establish that continuing colloquium, that never-ending conversation between Mark Hopkins and his publics, determined to modernize Mark Hopkins without changing one whit the essential characteristics of the learning process, determined through your public relations and development offices thus to preserve by means of a strong higher educational system the wisdom and the values without which our best American traditions cannot be handed on to the generations who will come after us.

*Delivered at the Greenbriar Conference, White Sulphur Springs, West Virginia, February 1958.*

# 13

# New Frontiers
# in Educational Finance

Not so very long ago Mark Van Doren wrote that "The experience that makes the deepest difference in any boy or girl is the experience of going to college. It is there that the man, the woman, is created; for it is there that thinking begins, and in our society there is no more noticeable difference than the difference between the thoughtful and the unthoughtful person. The difference has been called magic. There is no exaggeration in the term; it refers to the change from child to complete human being, the change that all of us desire insofar as we comprehend that the specific, the distinguishing quality of any person is the quality of his mind."[1]

Today I want to refer to that experience that makes the deepest difference in any boy or girl. I want to reflect briefly upon the most important element in that experience (the teacher), and I want primarily to discuss with you how we can make it possible to enrich that experience for the youth of America during the decade ahead.

I said I wanted to talk about the most important element in the college experience, the college professor, because he is the key man in America's future. Everything I have to say this morning will be directed to assuring the future of the heart and soul of our colleges and universities, the professor. The professor is the custodian of the treasured wisdom of the past; he is the idea man for the future, but he is something infinitely more important. He speaks with authority in his field of knowledge. His students respect his learning. His influence grows. His ideals, his values are transmitted almost unconsciously to his students. The college professor finds himself with a frightening power at his disposal—the power to shape a young life for time and eternity. This power is one of the most wonderful rewards of teaching. But how important also that he be a responsible moral person, one who reverences the thrill of guiding young minds and hearts. He can discharge his God-given task only in college or university setting where he can dedicate himself to his work, with the necessary resources for learning and teaching in the libraries and laboratories at his disposal, where in his own life and that of his family he can enjoy a well-founded sense of the respect, the support, the security, and the appreciation which is accorded to him by those who recognize the tremendous contribution he is making to the common weal. Yes, the college professor is today the key man in America's future.

How can we see to it that he can continue to perform his task in a decade which will see two students everywhere we see one today? How can we provide him with the environment, with the tools in the form of books and equipment which he needs if American higher education is to maintain its present quality and break through to new levels of excellence? How can we guarantee that the youth of America now in our elementary schools will share that "experience that makes the deepest difference . . . the experience of going to college" in a way that will provide our nation with the quality and quantity of educated citizens who alone can preserve our democratic way of life?

It is my firm conviction that we can and will furnish higher education in the necessary quantity and quality to the youth of America. It is by opening up new frontiers in educational finance that we will obtain the funds to assure the future of the college professors. It is by exploring these frontiers of educational finance that we will give to American youth that "experience that makes the deepest difference." I have begun this address by pointing out the importance of the college experience and the key part played by the professor in that experience because of my conviction that these are the really important things. The financial aspects of higher education, far from being ends in themselves, are nothing more than the necessary means for accomplishing the task.

Let us explore together the financial frontiers of American higher education to determine how we can best accomplish the Herculean task ahead of us. Let me preface my remarks by saying that $9 billion will be needed to keep the nation's higher education in high gear by 1970 compared with about $3.5 billion that we spend each year at present. You all know the reasons for the increase: a doubling of students and a required absolute minimum increase of 50 per cent in salaries for faculty members. Add to this the effects of inflation and the building facilities needed to handle the tidal wave of students and you have the main lines of the picture. Even so, we will still be spending only a little more than one per cent of our Gross National Product for higher education. Who should pay for all of this? The individual or society? As I hope to bring out, and as I am sure you already realize, the answer is a combination of both. The demands upon higher education in the future mean that higher education must be considered as a full-scale economic activity in which we must compete with other activities for the dollar.

The first frontier which I would like to explore with you is not a distant one, although for many of us it is an unknown frontier. It is the frontier of our own institutions. How can we increase the efficiency of our institutions without sacrificing the quality of education we offer? Is it possible to increase the quality with less expenditure? Our financial needs and our development programs are forcing us to scrutinize our ivory towers with a most critical eye. Does the student-teacher ratio have anything more to offer than a strong tradition? Or can we actually improve the quality of teaching by increasing this ratio? Can we justify every course that is offered? Can we justify giving it as often as we do? Could we improve the quality of our undergraduate programs by cooperative efforts with other colleges, similar to the program for science students at Argonne National Laboratory sponsored by the Associated Colleges of the Midwest? Do we know in which subjects we can teach large sections of 150 or more without harming quality? How can we improve our scheduling for the better use of classroom space? Can we honestly seek capital funds if our laboratories are vacant all morning and our classrooms are empty on Tuesdays and Thursdays? Should we explore the trimester operation as more in keeping with our urban society than the two-semester system adopted by an agricultural society? Can we improve our housekeeping to make our operations more efficient? Or should we spend more on upkeep to prevent expensive repairs in the future? These questions touch on the frontier closest to home and we must explore this frontier first of all. Only after exploring it carefully are we free to look toward other horizons.

The second frontier for the future financing of higher education is also close to home. It is the very sizeable item of tuition income. At present and into the foreseeable future there will always be a differential between the public and the private institution. Seymour Harris, the Harvard economist who has been making a national study of the economics of higher education, says that tuition in all institutions will rise substantially to provide us annually with $3.8 billion or 40 per cent of the amount needed for higher education, compared with the 25 per cent of the total provided by tuition at the present time. While I am not certain that students can be expected to provide an amount as great as this, it is my firm conviction that students must carry their fair share of the real cost of their education. In 1957, President Eisenhower's Committee on Education Beyond the High School, of which I was privileged to be a member, pointed out: "At present salary levels the teacher in effect subsidizes the education of the individual student and the benefits that society derives therefrom . . . an average salary structure approximately competitive with comparable professions would cost over $800 million in additional payroll annually. That is roughly the size of the present subsidy of higher education by its faculties in a single year." In such circumstances it is certainly fair to expect the student to assume a larger share of the real cost of his education and to provide his professors with a recompense to which they have a right and which will be sufficient to attract capable young men and women into the teaching profession.

Fortunately new attitudes on this frontier are rapidly developing. With a substantial boost from the National Defense Education Act Student Loan Program, it is now recognized as proper to obtain one's education on the installment plan, just as we purchase our homes, our automobiles, and so many other things in American life. More and more parents are coming to use the long-term pre-payment idea which insurance companies are now advocating. Banks are beginning to recognize the student as a good loan risk. Various tax credit plans for parents of college students are far from being a dead issue. Part-time employment, if limited in amount, can be of considerable financial assistance to students in urban colleges and universities. The number of scholarships is increasing but we must be conscious that such programs are of no assistance to the institution or its faculty unless they are accompanied by a cost-of-education grant to the institution. For this reason I feel that any increase in government assistance to higher education should give priority to assisting the institution, rather than the individual student, unless such a scholarship program includes a cost-of-education grant to the college or university.

During the years ahead we must bring home to our students the fact that their education is being subsidized by many sources and that as alumni they must expect to contribute to the education of the next generation. At Saint Louis University we have initiated an annual Student Endowment Day as an adjunct to our alumni Living Endowment Program and it has proved most successful in making students conscious of the extent of financial assistance they receive. I am confident that we will see in the decade ahead many new developments on the frontier of student fees.

The third frontier is that of planning. I am referring not only to institutional planning but to regional and state planning. Here in California, planning in the public institutions is ahead of that in most states. But there is urgent need throughout the country for regional and state planning commissions, recognized by law and financed by funds from the state and from business and labor organizations. These regional and state planning agencies should include both public and private institutions. They should study the needs of the area, evaluate the total resources available in present educational facilities, and the expected enlargement of such resources in the future. Institutions must learn to work together in planning cooperative programs, in eliminating duplication of offerings where this is possible. Surely it is unwise for all institutions to attempt to offer detailed courses in all areas of knowledge. Out of such planning agencies have come significant master plans for higher education and state-wide scholarship programs similar to the one which has been so successful in the state of California. One important by-product of such planning activity is the recognition on the part of both public and private institutions that our common traits and aims and objectives are far more numerous than we had imagined. A common understanding grows up which is important for higher education as a whole.

Recently McGraw-Hill Book Company sponsored a seminar on financing higher education in the coming decade and, while those present disagreed on many things, they were unanimous in this:

> that it would be a certain route to disaster all around for institutions operating under different kinds of sponsorship, such as public and private sponsorship, to divert energies badly needed for a common assault on their financial problems to slugging each other. There is, it was agreed, much room for constructive competition . . . but when, as it has on occasion, this rivalry descends below a plane of fair competition toward mutual questioning of educational good faith, there was complete agreement that mutual disaster is also being courted.

We have just begun to explore the frontier of inter-institutional and regional and state planning for higher education and I am confident that we will see development in this area parallel to the tremendous amount of regional and state planning carried out in relation to hospital facilities and the Hill-Burton Act.

The next frontier I want to explore with you is one where I am beginning to feel very much at home. It is the frontier of alumni support and corporate and philanthropic giving. On this frontier I feel a real kinship with Father Ledesma and the other early Jesuits, including our Founder, St. Ignatius himself. Many of you will recall, I am sure, that St. Ignatius did a good bit of begging in his lifetime and, to finance his own education at the University of Paris, he spent the summers begging in Holland and England. When he founded the Society of Jesus and wrote its Constitutions, he required endowment funds for the establishment of colleges and stipulated that the education was to be provided to students tuition-free. Modern conditions, of course, have forced a change in this, but it is interesting to note that the change did not officially take place until 1833, and only after Bishop Rosati of St. Louis asked Pope Gregory XVI to change the Jesuit rule. American Jesuits saw the crying need for education but could not find benefactors to endow the institutions that were so desperately needed.

St. Ignatius gave all Jesuits a rule that they must "beg from door to door whenever obedience or necessity requires it." I used to think this rule was just a historical curiosity until I became President of the University. However, I am able to console myself with the thought that my principal occupation during these weeks of the spring semester is very much in the tried and true Jesuit tradition, and I don't know another college or university president in America who is not similarly engaged.

One thing is abundantly clear about educational fund-raising at the present time. It is still very much a new and relatively unexplored frontier. Even institutions which have been engaged in fund-raising among alumni and corporations for twenty-five or thirty years realize that we have just begun to scratch the surface.

Let me lay down first of all a fundamental principle: If a good portion of our new income must come from sources outside the institution such as business and industry, we must present a business-like case to them. Once convinced of the great need for increased financial support for higher education they are willing to do their share. It is trite but true that fund-raising is fundamentally "friend-raising" and as such is the work of everyone who represents the college or university; the trustees, the president, the administrative officers, faculty, students, parents of students, alumni leaders of business and industry who know and understand the work of the institution. Alumni giving in recent years has shown a gratifying increase but there is still a long way to go. The record of $25 million a year given by one million of the approximately five million alumni solicited leaves ample room for improvement.

Corporate giving which in recent years has become one of the most important sources of added revenue, brings in about $150 million annually according to the Council for Financial Aid to Education. A great many organizations now generally recognize a responsibility to help maintain the kind of free society which enables them to prosper.

G. Keith Funston, formerly president of the New York Stock Exchange told a group of businessmen in Akron that

> there has been a tendency when examining the trend of corporate giving to label it 'public service' and let it go at that. It suggests a kind of 'do good' attitude on the part of management, and it overlooks the fact that companies are very specifically and directly involved in the fate of our colleges.
>
> The fact is that management sees industry growing because the economy is free—and colleges are both the well-spring and the conscience of freedom. It is not surprising that industry wants to protect that freedom, and that management is convinced that colleges will help do the job.
>
> . . . Industry today is critically short of the kind of people it will take to build tomorrow's world. There is real concern that, as our economic needs increase, the supply of college-trained manpower may be sadly inadequate.

Laws now enable corporations to give to philanthropic causes five per cent of their income before taxes which means that currently 52 per cent of a gift would otherwise be tax money. Just recently, in making a gift to Saint Louis University, a leading St. Louisan who is one of the nation's largest manufacturers of military equipment, wrote: "It will be helpful to the survival of our whole system of freedom if during the years to come all business organizations gradually become educated to the understanding that utilizing the full five per cent is to the best interest of the employees, is to the best interest of the shareholders, and is to the best interest of the customers, because all of them want our system of freedom to survive, and corporate giving is financially one of the most efficient ways to give."

At present corporations contribute about one-third of one per cent of income before taxes to education. A new movement has begun in Cleveland, called the Cleveland Compact, whereby corporations pledge to contribute a minimum of one per cent of their income before taxes to higher education. At the last available report, 21 corporations in the Cleveland area had joined the Compact and the movement is spreading to other cities. The Cleveland Compact, if widely adopted, would increase corporate giving to higher education from $150 million to almost half a billion dollars a year. This is just one example of the type of thinking which will open up whole new frontiers in the annual giving programs.

The last frontier in educational finance that I would like to explore with you is that of public support of higher education at the state and national levels. State support varies significantly from one part of the country to another and I will confine my remarks on it to a few brief comments. Seymour Harris and other experts do not expect an increase in state support of higher education nearly proportionate to the general rise in costs over the next ten years. The reasons vary considerably but many of them are related to the already heavy burden of elementary and secondary school taxes, to the outmoded tax base in most states, and the reluctance of state legislatures dominated by agricultural interests to alter this base or to vote the necessary funds for higher education. Coupled with this is a fear of driving industry out of the state by taxes that are excessively high. During the next ten years it is probable that state contributions to higher education will rise only $600 million, far short of the proportionate increase needed.

This means that a substantial portion of the increased support for American higher education must be sought from the federal public sector of the economy. If we are to maintain quality in the face of rising enrollments and rising costs, we must think of seeking about $2.7 billion annually from the federal government by 1970.

In the final analysis, the responsibility for education rests upon the people of America and while it is true that the time-honored American tradition calls for local and voluntary aid, experience shows that no matter how much they profit from or depend on higher education, some Americans will not do their share in supporting our institutions on a voluntary basis. The national interest demands that greater responsibility be assumed by organized government payments. This is one way in which they discharge their responsibility. It is not a long stride toward the welfare state.

Twice during the past year I have had this fact brought forcefully home to me. Last May it was my privilege to participate in the Seventeenth American Assembly at Arden House on the topic, "The Federal Government and Higher Education." Sixty persons representing every segment of American life assembled for a four-day discussion of this topic. Businessmen particularly arrived with one thought uppermost in their minds: Not one cent from the federal coffers should be given to higher education. But almost without exception during these discussions, those most opposed to federal aid became its most avid supporters. As one gentleman told me, "This is my first opportunity to discuss this problem with educators and I now realize that they have real problems which are national problems. There simply isn't any alternative to increased federal aid. I didn't know how much federal assistance there is already, nor did I appreciate before all the safeguards that exist to prevent federal control."

Last October Saint Louis University was host to one of the regional assemblies on the same topic. We brought in businessmen and labor leaders and housewives, professional and military men and educators from fourteen midwestern states and exactly the same reaction took place. This convinced me that much of the opposition to increased federal support for higher education is based on simple lack of knowledge. For instance, most people do not realize that present federal assistance amounts to about half a billion dollars a year, that total expenditures for the GI Bill and related legislation have come to more than $14 billion. People do not realize that the federal government was assisting education even before the Northwest Ordinance of 1787. They have forgotten the Morrill Act of 1862 and its continuing effects.

The question at issue is not whether the federal government should have a role in higher education. That was settled affirmatively in the nineteenth century and has not been reopened. The question is *what kind* of role the government should assume.

So-called fears about federal control can best be allayed, I think, by reference to an address delivered at the Midwest Assembly by Alan Waterman, director of the National Science Foundation, whose long experience in the field of federal aid to education has been tested and found true. He said,

> For the future, two things seem clear: one is that there will have to be a steady increase in federal expenditures for higher education if we are to meet the needs of the space age; the other is that there must be every effort to increase the funds available from all sources in order that the universities may achieve a balanced support . . . so far as federal support of higher education is concerned, we are probably at about the same stage now that we were with respect to federal support of basic research in the early post-war years. At that time a number of people in the universities and colleges viewed this new development with misgivings. . . . As time went on, however, government and university people worked closely together to develop procedures for the support of research through contracts and grants that have overcome practically all of the initial reservations of academic people. There are still problems to be solved—indirect costs, for example—but today virtually all of the universities and colleges are not only willing but anxious to receive funds for the support of basic research . . . there is now very little

concern that the federal government is likely to take over control of university research.

There are four principles in appraising federal aid, according to the Rockefeller Report, which I shall summarize this way: First, only high priority needs should be government supported. Secondly, we must remember that federal funds are only one support among many kinds. State, local and private funds should still be the major source of financing education. Third, government aid should preserve local leadership and control over education, and finally the government must be aware of, and exercise its function as, a leader, a pacemaker.

Much of what now is considered federal aid is really the purchase of services and for this the government should pay the full cost, including the full cost of institutional overhead. Other programs such as those for student housing and boarding facilities are really loans and not federal aid.

I agree wholeheartedly with President David D. Henry of the University of Illinois who recently declared: "I share the view that private institutions must receive some form of public support if we are going to maintain a first-rate system of higher education, widely accessible to all students, with the research and service roles strong . . . In the long history of federal grants, the precedents are ample for aiding institutions and organizations, whether public or private, which are operating in the national welfare."[2]

We need only cite the NYA program of the 1930s, surplus property distribution, the GI Bill, and the present policies of the National Science Foundation and the National Institute of Health.

In any new program of federal aid, top priority should be given to the provision of matching grants to all institutions for the construction of academic facilities. This suggestion is hardly a new one. In fact, it has been a considerable disappointment to those of us who were members of President

Eisenhower's Committee on Education Beyond the High School that Congress did not formally consider our recommendation for grants of this type. The committee assigned three reasons for these grants which I think are worthy of note: "It would help institutions to concentrate more on financing adequate facilities. It can be terminated when enrollments level off, without disrupting institutions' current finances. It contains little, if any, possibility of federal control of educational programs."

We must spend about $1.3 billion each year through 1970 for capital construction in order to handle the doubling enrollments. A federal program of matching grants of $750 million a year for ten years would stimulate local matching grants and would enable us to provide for the tremendous enrollment increases which have already begun. It would also enable us to up-date some of our present facilities which have long been obsolete.

It is interesting to note that in a recent poll among members of the Association of American Colleges, a solid 84 per cent of those responding strongly endorsed a program of federal matching grants for academic facilities, with government loans as alternative forms of assistance at the option of the individual institution.

While I did not select the title of this address with President Kennedy's campaign theme in mind, I am, nevertheless, pleased that the frontier of greater public support for higher education will be explored by Congress so early in his administration.

We return now to our starting point. By imaginative exploration of these financial frontiers I am confident that we will provide the means which are so desperately needed to achieve a breakthrough to new levels of excellence in American higher education. Without exploration of these financial frontiers, we are doomed to mediocrity. With such exploration we will be able to attract and hold college professors, the key men in America's future. We will be in the best possible position to provide a quality education to the youth of America, that "experience of going to college, the experience that makes the deepest difference."

*Delivered at Loyola University, Los Angeles, California, February 20, 1961.*

## NOTES

1. Leaflet published by American Textbook Publishers Institute, New York.
2. David D. Henry "Federal Responsibility in Higher Education," *The Federal Governmnet and Higher Education: The Saint Louis University Midwest Assembly,* pp. 13, 15.

# 14

## Five Big Questions in Higher Education

Even those closest to the situation are not fully aware of the phenomenal changes that are taking place in higher education in the United States. These changes are lightning-like in their rapidity and colossal in their implications both for American educational philosophy and for the practical "nuts and bolts" of higher education. Frank Keppel said in a recent feature article in *Time* "what we don't know about American education will hurt us." At the present moment, the changes are taking place so rapidly that educators are incapable of formulating the important questions to be asked. Even more impossible is the task of discovering the right answers to these big questions.

You, as men and women who are responsible for the alumni activities, the public relations offices, and the fund-raising activities of many of our colleges and universities, share with administrators and faculty members the responsibility of making yourself fully aware of these questions. My objective is to discuss what some of the biggest of these questions seem to be, and to suggest tentative answers as I see them at this moment. If such questions are already being discussed at your institution, then I would hope that you are involved in this discussion and are contributing what you can toward developing the right answers to them. If, on the other hand, these questions are not being discussed at your college or university, I would submit that you would be making a major contribution to the future of the institution by raising them.

*Question number one:* To what extent should our colleges and universities be free to determine their own purposes and objectives, and to what extent should these be political decisions?

The Higher Education Act of 1965, signed by President Johnson on November 8, is a culmination point in a rapidly crystallizing relationship between the higher educational establishment and the Federal Government. During the past few years, of course, we came to the startling realization that perhaps fifty to one hundred of the largest, most complex universities were being influenced tremendously in their policies, their research, their financing, etc., by reason of the fact that as much as fifty to seventy-five percent of their total operational budget was coming from federal sources. Even smaller institutions found themselves developing new departments or strengthening others in order to conform to various types of financial assistance made available by the National Defense Education Act as amended in 1964. Peter Miurhead, associate commissioner in the U.S. Office of Education, argues that with the Higher Education Act of 1965 the policy of the Federal Government toward higher education has now developed into a mosaic in which the myriad pieces of legislation are being fitted together into a single piece. While this simile is not out of place, the mosaic of federal relationships to higher education at the present moment scarcely resembles an early historical type of mosaic in which a theme was presented in clear-cut proportions and with unity throughout. Rather, it has many of the qualities of modernistic mosaics where the meaning, as well as the unity of the composition, is not too obvious.

I am not necessarily criticizing the fact that government money will now be available to most institutions for almost any type of program which they normally sponsor. Rather, what I am saying is that now as never before we must be on our guard lest we allow this financial assistance to shape our educational policies and mar the unique character of each of our institutions.

*Question number two:* In view of the fact that governmental assistance to higher education across the board is at least tacitly recognized in the Higher Education Act of 1965, would it not be better for all of us to back up long enough to redefine the rationale for government assistance?

Initially, government assistance to higher education was on a "quid pro quo" basis—e.g., research efforts in order to assist the government to find an answer to a problem of special interest. Such defense-influenced legislation resulted in the Atomic Energy Commission (1946) and the National Science Foundation (1950). Even in the case of governmental assistance for the improvement of faculties and instructional facilities, the rationale was placed in the area of the importance of these developments for the defense of our country hence the amended NDEA (1964) and the Higher Education Facilities Act (1963). At this point in our history, I would argue that it makes more sense to attempt to re-define the rationale of government assistance by stating that there is a higher political validity to the financing of the general intellectual development of our American people rather than to the support of practical and applied functions of education. If those of us responsible for the continuing development of our colleges and universities do not ask and help to

formulate answers to these fundamental questions, our relationship with the Federal Government is almost certainly
doomed to become an increasingly complicated mess, a relationship that is wasteful because of duplications in administrative functions, competition between governmental agencies,
opportunities for the creation of unnecessary positions, and
wastage of all kinds. We must work to simplify our relationships with the Federal Government by clarifying and purify-
ing the basic reason for government aid, the raising of the
general level of intelligence of our citizens.

*Question number three:* In view of current developments,
how valid is the age-old distinction between public and private
higher education?

Because of the rapidly increasing costs of carrying on and
expanding the higher education establishment, institutions
supported by state and local taxes are securing smaller proportions of their total operating budget from taxes. More and
more, they are looking toward corporate and private philanthropy for supplementary funds. On the other hand, now
that the Higher Education Act is the law of the land, private
colleges and universities will be participating in federal funds
both for operational and capital expenditures. The trend,
obviously, is in the direction of erasing the rather sharp line
that used to divide the two types. If this is true, I would
suggest that this has tremendous implications for you who
are specialists in the field of public relations. Must you not
rethink what has been so glibly said and written about the
differences in days past? The appeal to businessmen, for
example, that private colleges are the stronghold of private
enterprise and the bulwark against creeping socialism loses
most of whatever "punch" it may have had when both types
of institutions are being supported by the same categories of
givers.

Tremendous also are the implications for those of you who
are interested in alumni giving and fund-raising generally.
What answers will you give to the alumnus of a private col-

lege or to the president of a corporation who indicates that he is no longer interested in giving at all, or at least not as much, in view of the fact that his alma mater, or the private college in question, now shares in the benefits of the public trough? The answer to this question can be given adequately only in a carefully phrased statement by one who really understands how federal assistance programs actually come into being. Take the genesis of Title II of the Facilities Act. Leaders in higher education pointed out to the United States Office of Education that one of the most seriously needed yet most difficult type of facility to provide was a building for graduate instruction and research. Typically, such facilities serve a relatively smaller number of students than undergraduate facilities; they are not income-producing; they are particularly expensive, often requiring sophisticated equipment and installations for advanced research, etc. With the advice of experts in graduate education, a program to meet this real need was formulated and eventually became law. A highly respected educator, the Dean of the Graduate School at the University of Indiana, Dr. John Ashton, was employed to head this Title II program. An advisory committee largely composed of educators was established as part of the legislation. This committee formulated the procedural regulations. When an application has been submitted, the institution receives a site visit by one or more members of the committee and a staff person. They make a recommendation to a panel of educators who have been chosen because they are well-informed in particular fields—library, natural science, teacher education, etc. Finally, the total advisory committee considers the application directly, reviews the reports of the site visitors and the panel, and then agrees to approve or withhold the grant, a decision that must be followed by the United States Office of Education. By and large, it is simply not true that federal assistance programs in education are managed and controlled by federal bureaucrats, but with public opinion to the contrary in many quarters, we have a tremendous job of education to achieve before the average citizen understands this. Surely this a very important responsibility of the public relations officers of our colleges and universities.

*Question number four:* Are you fully aware of the far-reaching consequences of the fantastic change in the relation between the total enrollments of private colleges and universities as compared with those of public institutions?

Although the situation varies from state to state, the prediction seems sound that, in the very near future, 80 or 85 per cent of all the boys and girls in post-high school education will be enrolled in a tax-supported institution of one kind or another. If this is true, then obviously both private and public higher education should pause long enough to examine and re-define their respective roles. It would seem obvious that in the vast panoply of post-high-school education there are some roles which are no longer appropriate for most private institutions.

Again, since many private institutions will probably remain in the smaller category insofar as size is concerned, surely this demands that they make a careful scrutiny as to what kinds of education, what types of curricula, etc., they can best offer, and what they, as smaller private institutions, can do as a *unique* contribution to our educational resources. You should be playing an important role in determining and then publicizing what your college or university is committed to accomplish as its unique, clearly defined, but nevertheless very important contribution to the total higher educational needs of this country.

*Question number five:* How is the higher educational establishment to be financed? More specifically, how and in what proportions should this financing be shared by: (a) the individual beneficiary of education, (b) private philanthropists, and (c) the political community?

Probably the biggest question of all in higher education today is what in the long run should be the pattern of support for private as well as public colleges and universities. I have here, for example, the percentages of income from various sources allocated by both private and public universities towards financing their 1963–1964 operating budgets.[1] Let's start with the percentage of current-fund income that is realized from the student and his parents in the form of tuition and fees. For public universities this source constituted only 10.2 per cent of the total budget; for private, only 25 per cent. These figures say a number of things. First of all, it is clear that in neither public nor private institutions have our tuition fees remotely kept pace with the spiralling costs of educating those who pay these fees. This is a fact which the general public still does not understand or believe—another unfinished task for our public relations departments. Secondly, these figures again raise the question of the widening gap between tuition charges in private as contrasted with public institutions. I used to argue for the imperative need for community and state colleges and universities to raise their tuition charges. I still think this would be wise, but I have now resigned myself to the fact that it is not going to happen, with the exception of increased charges on out-of-state students. There is an overwhelming majority of the American public which is committed to the idea that the opportunity for free education, at least through the four-year college level, is the right of our American youth. With low-cost collegiate education becoming available through the junior college and community college explosion, it is abundantly clear that private colleges, faced with the necessity of getting at least that 25 per cent of their operating income from tuition, can compete for students, especially good students, only if they can mount a massive program of financial assistance to those who otherwise could not attend such an institution. I will say something about governmental scholarship and loan programs a little later on, but at this point I want to voice my conviction that from now on the fund-raising programs of private colleges will have to include much larger amounts for student-aid programs of various kinds.

In 1963–64, the public universities received 61.1 per cent
of their total operating budget from the state and federal
government; from these sources the private institutions received 35.9 per cent (mostly, of course, from the Federal
Government). Any source that provides from one-third to
two-thirds of an operating budget is tremendously important,
and therefore the cultivation of governmental resources by our
public relations and fund-raising departments, especially in
our private institutions, must become a much more important
priority than it is in most of them today. I think I could
document the statement that very few small private colleges
are really exploiting the governmental resources that are
available to them. For example, there is a Small Grants Program in the U.S. Office of Education which is looking for
applicants. Some colleges are getting as much as $50,000 a
year in grants for their faculty and students; most colleges
don't even know the program exists.

From now on, of course, one of the major boosts to our
operational income from government will come in the form of
scholarships as well as loans for our students. Here again one
of your increasingly important tasks is not only to make certain that accurate information about these student-aid programs is made easily available to prospective students and
their parents, but also you must prevent or correct much
misinformation currently abroad about these programs. For
example, some of your trustees, some of the leading businessmen in your city, are convinced from reading local press
releases that the new loan program in the Higher Education
Act is going to ruin the private loan programs sponsored by
or guaranteed by local banks. The facts of the case, however,
are these. Some years ago the United Student Aid Funds, Inc.
was established to create a privately financed loan program
for students. It was designed to meet a crying need and one
which many were convinced should not be met only by governmental sources through NDEA loans. United Student Aid
Funds guarantees the private loans made to students by local

banks. When it appeared that the new legislation in the Higher Education Act might include a provision for the United States Government to guarantee student loans, the Board of the United Student Aid Funds, of which I am a member, gathered enough support to convince Washington that this would not be a wise move. Accordingly, the new law actually protects private loan funds by stating that the government loan program is strictly a "back-up" program to be implemented only when there is no private or state program reasonably available to a student. Here is a very important public information assignment for you to undertake.

Although we have been talking about state and federal governmental support of our annual budget, I want to interject just one thought about governmental aid programs for capital expenditures. Public relations and development staffs should exert every effort to keep up to the minute in this area which is evolving and becoming more important almost by the minute. To give but one example, the officially designated agency in each state is empowered within general guidelines to determine the procedures by means of which applicants in the state qualify for matching construction funds under Title I of the College Facilities Act. It is no secret that in some states the formulae originally developed are working to the disadvantage of, if not with real injustice towards, some types of collegiate institutions in that state. How much do you know about the situation in your state as it affects your school? If it isn't what it should be, what are you doing to create a body of public opinion that will lead to a more equitable procedure for the allotting of these governmental funds?

There is one more area which falls under governmental assistance in which I feel that public relations and development personnel have a duty which is generally being neglected. I am speaking of state scholarship programs. If you haven't read it, please read the article in the current (Fall) issue of ACPRA's *College and University Journal* by a member of our faculty, Dr. Daniel D. McGarry, professor of history. Directly, Dr. McGarry devotes the entire article to a detailed description of the nature, procedures, accomplishments, and advantages of the student-aid program in the State of New York. But indirectly and more importantly, Dr. McGarry provides those of us in the 35 states that have no scholarship program with some powerful arguments for rallying public opinion, including our trustees, faculty, alumni, students, parents, etc., in favor of establishing such a scholarship program. Moreover, his article clearly indicates why some state programs are much more effective and equitable than others. You should be interested in knowing that Kansas is the only state in your eight-state area that has had a scholarship program for several years and that Iowa just this year put such a program into legislation. What we need far more than buildings are capable, eager students even if they be financially handicapped. Nothing is more important, therefore, for you who are charged with the responsibility of helping to secure essential support for your institution, than to participate in an on-going, well-designed public relations program to bring about the establishment or the improvement and expansion of a scholarship program in your state.

A third area of support for their operating expenditures came to the public and private universities from *private philanthropy*—private gifts and grants. In this category, I think it is important to realize that this source took care of only 2.9 per cent of the current-fund income of public and only 8.8 per cent of the private institutions. Much of the money from corporations, foundations, alumni and friends has been going ino capital expenditures, especially for the new facilities needed as we expand our enrollments. But I think the moment of truth is approaching for many of us, particularly those in the private sector. To balance our budgets as instructional salaries and general educational costs continue to spiral, I suspect we will have to look to private philanthropy to carry a larger share of the operational burden. This means that many of us may have to slow down our physical expansion; this may mean revising our enrollment projections downward; this will certainly mean that you in public relations and development departments will have to devise new approaches—I don't want to say "gimmicks"—to attract the private dollar.

Not only must we learn to interest prospective donors in the operational budget in contrast to the more attractive lure of a lasting memorial in stone or brick and mortar; we may even have to think of ways in which to encourage giving in order to avoid deficits, and to devise an attractive "come-on" for alumni and friends to pay back debts. We all know about the problems recently encountered by the University of Pittsburgh where, in spite of dynamic leadership and fund-raising success that evoked jealousy on the part of many of us, this university found itself stifled with a $19.5 million accumulated deficit. Now, instead of long-range development plans, Edgar B. Cale, Vice Chancellor for Development, has started a campaign to secure unrestricted contributions from alumni. "It's perhaps not satisfying," he says, "for alumni to give money to pay bills, but that's our best use for gifts now." And Pitt may end up as another in a growing list of private institutions which, though actually quite vigorous and dynamic in their growth, have been forced, because of creeping indebtedness, to turn to the legislature and ask to become part of the state system. Here, surely, is an almost frightening challenge for those of you in private colleges and universities. Are you going to be ingenious enough to win the kind of unrestricted money your institution needs to operate on a balanced budget year in and year out? Getting an overdose of capital funds may be very exciting and impressive but you may only be helping to dig the grave of still another private institution.

I've asked you five very serious questions tonight—

1) What decisions should our institutions make for them-selves; what decisions should be made by government?
2) What should be the fundamental rationale for government aid to higher education?
3) Today, how valid are the old distinctions between public and private institutions?
4) What should be the role of private colleges in the light of changing conditions?
5) How is higher education, both public and private, to be financed?

I have attempted to give you a few tentative, far-from-certain answers to these huge questions. Even though I am not sure of these answers, there is one thing I am sure of: to find the definite answers and to put them into practical ap-plication in our colleges and universities in the days ahead, you public relations, alumni, and development officers will have to shake off the old stereotyped programs and ways of doing your job and discover some new, untapped sources of gifts, and some ingenious, creative methods of interesting all of our publics in far greater support of all forms of higher education than has ever been realized up to now. In a word, yours is a gigantic task, and my advice to you is: you can't take it on too quickly.

*Delivered before the American College Public Relations Associa-tion-American Alumni Council, November 1965.*

## NOTE

1. As chairman of the Association of American Colleges' Commis-sion on College and Society, the writer is greatly indebted to its mem-bers for many of the ideas expressed in this paper. A statement on these basic questions was first introduced into the discussion of the Com-mission by President Thomas A. Spragens, President of Centre College, Danville, Kentucky.